ARTHUR RATHGEBER/SANDRA RATHGEBER
STUDY GUIDE

FIFTH EDITION

EXCEPTIONAL CHILDREN

Introduction to Special Education

HALLAHAN

KAUFFMAN

PRENTICE HALL, Englewood Cliffs, N.J. 07632

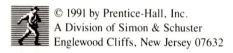 © 1991 by Prentice-Hall, Inc.
A Division of Simon & Schuster
Englewood Cliffs, New Jersey 07632

Production supervision: Tally Morgan, WordCrafters Editorial Services, Inc.
Buyers: D. Kesar/M. Gloriande
Supplemental acquisitions editor: S. Chambliss
Acquisitions editor: C. Wada
Cover designer: Florence Silverman

Printed in the United States of America

10 9 8 7 6 5 4 3 2 1

ISBN 0-13-293358-6

Prentice-Hall International (UK) Limited, *London*
Prentice-Hall of Australia Pty. Limited, *Sydney*
Prentice-Hall Canada Inc., *Toronto*
Prentice-Hall Hispanoamericana, S.A., *Mexico*
Prentice-Hall of India Private Limited, *New Delhi*
Prentice-Hall of Japan, Inc., *Tokyo*
Simon & Schuster Asia Pte. Ltd., *Singapore*
Editora Prentice-Hall do Brasil, Ltda., *Rio de Janeiro*

CONTENTS

AN INTRODUCTORY NOTE TO STUDENTS

This Study Guide is intended to assist you in focusing your attention on the major facts and concepts presented in the Textbook. It is our intention that *mastery* of these facts and concepts will be achieved as you become actively engaged with the exercises within the Study Guide. In addition to using the Textbook and the Study Guide, you will need a notebook in which to record many of your responses. These three pieces of material will be invaluable to you as you prepare for examinations.

Five features of this Study Guide will assist your interaction with the information in the Textbook. These features are:
1. A number of question types are presented. These questions address both the content of the chapter as well as the variety of learning styles of students.
2. Questions in each section are presented in the order in which the information appears in the Textbook.
3. Page numbers are provided at the conclusion of each question rather than within the Answer Key. This allows you to scan the appropriate section in the Textbook, in order to check for the accuracy of your response rather than just utilizing the answer key.
4. Answers are provided for the Multiple Choice, True/False, Matching, and Fill-In-The-Blank sections. Answers are not provided for the Short Answer Questions, however, the accompanying page number will allow you to check the accuracy of your response. Responses to some of the *Understanding the Facts* and *Applying the Facts* questions will require the assistance of your instructor.
5. The Multiple Choice and Short Answer items are divided into three levels of learning: *Remembering the Facts*; *Understanding the Facts*; and *Applying the Facts*.

Remembering the Facts: These items test your recall of specific facts in the chapter. Students may find that some of these exercises require more searching for details than what may be required by an examination by the instructor. The reason for this emphasis is to provide more engaged time with the Textbook.

Understanding the Facts: These items test your understanding of the facts and concepts that are presented in the chapter.

Applying the Facts: These items represent a higher level of comprehension by questioning your interpretation and application of the facts and concepts.

This Study Guide contains a unit on each of the 11 chapters in the Textbook, all arranged with the following exercises: (1) Terminology; (2) Multiple Choice; (3) True and False; (4) Short Answer; (5) Fill-In-The-Blank; (6) Return to Chapter Summary; and (7) Enrichment. Some chapters also include a Matching exercise. Following are some comments regarding how to effectively use each of these exercises.

1. Terminology: This exercise is an introduction to key terms. It is recommended that you write a definition of each of these terms 'in your own words' in your Study Guide notebook. A Fill-In-The-Blank exercise, using each of these terms, is provided at the conclusion of each chapter in order to test your understanding of the key terminology.

2. Multiple Choice: The Multiple Choice items will assist with your mastery of the facts, understanding, evaluation, and application of the Textbook information.

3. Matching: Some concepts are more efficiently presented in a Matching format. In some chapters, it is a matching of *details,* whereas in other chapters you are required to match *applications.*

4. True and False: These items will assist in your understanding of the facts and applications of Textbook information in two ways. First of all, you will be required to indicate whether the statement is True or False. Second, it is suggested that you rewrite the False statements in order to make them accurate.

5. Short Answer Questions: Short answer questions require that you a) summarize; b) evaluate; c) analyze; and d) synthesize the material from the Textbook.

6. Fill-In-The-Blank: Terminology listed at the beginning of each chapter is put into a *scrambled* format so that you can test your understanding of these terms. Some of these items will be a straight-forward definition, however, most of the items will be in the form of a contextual situation in which you will be required to *understand* the definition in order to complete the item.

7. Return to Chapter Summary: At this point in your study, it would be effective to reread the summary of the chapter in the textbook. This summary provides the essence of the chapter that will assist in the integration of new information that has been presented. As the summary is reread, you should find yourself elaborating on the many points that are reviewed. This review and elaboration at this time will strengthen your mastery of the concepts learned. Read slowly to allow yourself to consolidate your learning.

8. Enrichment Activities: These suggestions are provided with the intention of expanding your study beyond the Textbook. Some of these activities may also be used by your instructor to enrich the experience of the entire class.

SUGGESTIONS ON HOW TO APPROACH EACH CHAPTER

1. Chapter objectives are provided at the beginning of each chapter in the Study Guide. Read the Textbook chapter with the outlined objectives in mind.

2. At the conclusion of your initial reading, review each of the objectives. Attempt to write statements in your Study Guide notebook that begin to elaborate on each of the objectives.

3. Reread the chapter. Highlight main points and make some notes for yourself in your Study Guide notebook.

4. Complete the Study Guide exercises in the order of presentation. You may wish to use a pencil to record your responses in order that the responses can be erased. This will allow you to redo these exercises at examination time.

5. Return to the chapter objectives and determine your competence.

6. We recommend that this study process be followed before attending the lecture that corresponds with the chapter. During the lecture, you will be prepared to listen with more understanding, be more selective with note-taking, and be more directed in asking questions.

7. At examination time, reread your highlighted Textbook; reread your Study Guide notebook - paying special attention to the objectives; reread lecture notes; redo Fill-In-The-Blanks, Multiple Choice, Matching, and True/False Exercises. Test yourself by writing - from memory - several statements that elaborate on each of the objectives for the chapter.

Both of us recognize that understanding the issues in teaching exceptional children is a complex task. For this reason we have provided this format which allows numerous opportunities for you to master the knowledge in this area, as well as opportunities to gain inferential knowledge that is essential in order to be effective with exceptional students.

Sandra H. Rathgeber
Arthur J. Rathgeber

C H A P T E R

1

Exceptionality and Special Education

CHAPTER FOCUS

Chapter one introduces the study of exceptional children by emphasizing that the similarities among exceptional and nonexceptional individuals are more significant than the differences. This chapter provides general information about exceptional children and the special education programs that are available for them.

CHAPTER OBJECTIVES

On completion of this chapter, the student should be able to discuss the following topics:

1. The difference between a *disability* and a *handicap*
2. Definitions of *special education* and *exceptional children*
3. General statements about the prevalence of exceptional children
4. The various special education services available to all exceptional children
5. The roles of regular and special education teachers
6. The history of special education
7. The provisions of the three laws that are the foundation of special education services
8. Information to be included in an IEP
9. Current trends and issues in special education

1

TERMINOLOGY

Terms to Note:

The following terms are important to note. These terms will be used in a Fill-In-The-Blank exercise at the conclusion of this chapter.

1. disability (p.6)
2. handicap (p.6)
3. exceptional children (p.6)
4. prevalence (p.6)
5. special education (p.8)
6. least restrictive environment (p.11,12)
7. permissive legislation (p.22)
8. mandatory legislation (p.22)
9. PL 94-142 (p.22)
10. PL 99-457 (p.22)
11. Section 504 of PL 93-112 (p.23)
12. due process (p.24,25)
13. individualized education program (IEP) (p.25-30)
14. normalization (p.31)
15. integration (p.31)
16. cultural diversity (p.31)
17. early intervention (p.31)
18. transition (p.31)

MULTIPLE CHOICE

Select the most appropriate response.

A. Remembering The Facts

1. Hallahan and Kauffman state that the most important goal of special education is: (p.6)
    a. to provide appropriate instructional materials for exceptional learners.
    b. to instruct exceptional learners using appropriate methodology.
    c. to capitalize on the exceptional learner's abilities.
    d. to improve our psychological assessment techniques.

2. Which of the following statements is FALSE concerning the reasons why difficulty is encountered when counting exceptional children? (p.7)

   a. Many exceptional children have multiple disabilities.
   b. School performance is often a major criteria in determining an exceptionality.
   c. Definitions of exceptionalities are vague and are constantly changing.
   d. Assessment instruments and methods used to identify exceptional students are always reliable and valid.

3. According to the text, ___ of the North American student population have been identified as handicapped. This is the most current prevalence estimate for special education purposes. (p.2,7)

   a. five percent   d. 20 percent
   b. ten percent   e. 25 percent
   c. 15 percent

4. The most integrated intervention for exceptional children is ___. (p.8-10)

   a. the regular classroom   d. an itinerant program
   b. the resource room   e. a residential school
   c. a special classroom

5. The most segregated level of intervention for exceptional children is ___. (p.8-10)

   a. the regular classroom   d. an itinerant program
   b. the resource room   e. a residential school
   c. a special classroom

6. The placement of a child in a setting that is productive, consistent with needs, and is as normal as possible is known as ___. (p.11,12)

   a. the least restrictive environment
   b. the resource room
   c. special education
   d. a diagnostic-prescriptive center
   e. normalization

7. Special education's beginnings are rooted in___. (p.18-20)

   a. medicine   d. both b and c
   b. psychology/psychiatry   e. all of the above
   c. sociology and education

8. ____ is the individual to whom the beginnings of special education are attributed. (p.18)

    a. Seguin   c. Montessori
    b. Itard   d. Pinel

9. Which of the following special education pioneers was the founder of the Perkins School for the Blind? (p.19)

    a. Itard   c. Seguin
    b. Howe   d. Montessori

10. *Permissive* legislation concerning special education provisions in schools existed until ___. (p.22)

    a. 1954   c. 1975
    b. 1968   d. 1986

11. In ___ federal legislation concerning special education provisions to children aged three to five became *mandatory*. (p.22)

    a. 1954   c. 1975
    b. 1968   d. 1986

12. Another name for PL 94-142 is ___. (p.22)

    a. Education for All Handicapped Children Act
    b. Education for All Disabled Children Act
    c. Council for Exceptional Children
    d. Special Education Act

13. Which of the following pieces of information does NOT need to be included in an IEP? (p.25,26)

    a. family medical history
    b. student's present level of academic performance
    c. evaluation methods
    d. long-term and short-term goals
    e. the extent of mainstreaming efforts

14. Which of the following statements is TRUE? (p.33,35)

    a. Adolescents with mild disabilities usually drop out of school and become dependent upon their families.
    b. Adolescents with mild disabilities often do not receive the necessary help in adjusting to the demands of adulthood.
    c. Adolescents with moderate to severe disabilities often do not get the services they need to help them adjust to the demands of adulthood.
    d. Adolescents with moderate to severe disabilities have less difficulty locating and keeping a job than does an adolescent with mild disabilities.

B. Understanding The Facts

15. In which way(s) is Jim Abbott *exceptional*? (p.5,6)

    a. He is an incredibly good baseball player.
    b. He plays with an artificial hand.
    c. He has only one hand.
    d. a and c
    e. b and c

16. The term *handicapped* would apply to which population? (p.6)

    a. the intellectually gifted
    b. the severely retarded
    c. both a and b
    d. neither a nor b

17. The term *exceptional* would apply to which population? (p.6)

    a. the intellectually gifted
    b. the severely retarded
    c. both a and b
    d. neither a nor b

18. What would be one method of lowering the prevalence estimates for exceptional children? (p.7)

    a. improve teaching techniques
    b. increase school systems' special education budgets
    c. change the criteria for the definitions of exceptionalities
    d. utilize a wider variety of tests in identifying exceptional children

19. Which of the following special education services would be expected to have the highest 'price tag'? (p.8-10)

    a. regular classroom   d. residential school
    b. resource room   e. diagnostic-prescriptive
    c. self-contained class   center

20. Which of the following statements about the least restrictive environment is FALSE? (p.12)

   a. The exceptional child should spend at least part of the school day in a regular classroom.
   b. Segregation from peers should be as minimal as possible.
   c. The exceptional child should experience a normal lifestyle as much as possible.
   d. The educational program for exceptional children should be consistent with their needs.

21. According to PL 94-142, the cost of special education services are the responsibility of ___. (p.23,24)
   a. the child's family
   b. the federal government
   c. the state government and local school districts
   d. both a and c
   e. both b and c

C. Applying The Facts

22. George was identified as having auditory discrimination problems at the end of second grade. He is now achieving satisfactorily as a senior in high school. George's condition is now a ___. (p.6)

   a. handicap   b. disability

23. Which of the following exceptional children would probably be the LEAST likely to benefit from itinerant services? (p.8)

   a. speech and language impaired
   b. moderately mentally retarded
   c. visually impaired
   d. physically disabled

24. When should a student be referred for special education services? (p.14-16)

   a. only when the student's needs have not been successfully met in a regular class
   b. at the first sign of a learning challenge in the regular classroom
   c. when the student's achievement falls below the regular class average
   d. only when the teacher has noted significant behavior and academic problems

MATCHING

Match each of the following special education services with the appropriate defining characteristics. (p.8-10)

a. Regular Classroom
b. Consultation
c. Itinerant Teacher
d. Resource Teacher
e. Diagnostic-Prescriptive Center

f. Hospital/Homebound
g. Self-Contained Class
h. Special Day School
i. Residential School

1. ___ provides individual or small-group instruction on a regular basis in the classroom or in another room in one school
2. ___ suitable for mild exceptionalities; provides demonstration and instruction to assist the regular classroom teacher only when requested
3. ___ provides 24-hour care and instruction to exceptional children; suitable for severe exceptionalities
4. ___ does not require the services of a special education teacher; attempts to meet all academic/social needs of the students
5. ___ provides regular or intermittent instruction or consultation with students and/or teachers in several schools
6. ___ is useful for a student who is 'new' to special education; provides a comprehensive assessment of student's needs and an educational plan for instruction
7. ___ provides short-term instructional services to a student who has been temporarily withdrawn from school
8. ___ provides effective service for children with severe exceptionalities; special education teacher provides instruction in a segregated setting for the school day
9. ___ can be located in a community school; special education teacher provides all of the instruction; some social integration with the other classrooms may occur

TRUE AND FALSE

Indicate whether the following statements are True or False. In your notebook, rewrite the False statements so that they are accurate.

1. An exceptional child can *only* be defined as being different from the average child. (p.2)   T   F

2. The least restrictive environment for an exceptional child is generally considered to be the regular classroom. (p.3,11,12) T   F

3. All children must be provided with a free public education regardless of their handicap. (p.3,22)   T   F

4. Professionals almost always agree on the defining characteristics of exceptional children. (p.7)   T   F

5. Special education's history began in North America. (p.18) T   F

6. The first residential school for the deaf was the Perkins School. (p.19)   T   F

7. PL 99-457 provides legislation for exceptional children aged three to five. (p.22)   T   F

8. Federal, state, and local governments all share equally in the cost of funding special education programs. (p.24) T   F

9. Early intervention guarantees a decrease in the prevalence of disabilities among children. (p.32,33)   T   F

SHORT ANSWER QUESTIONS

Answer the following questions in your notebook.

A. Remembering The Facts

1. What reason do the authors suggest for the lack of specific statements defining exceptional children? (p.2)

2. Before any referral to special education services is made, what three actions must be taken? (p.15)

3. In your own words, list and briefly describe the eight responsibilities of *all* educators. (p.15,16)

4. Identify and briefly describe four specific expectations for special educators. (p.17)

5. For each of the following important individuals in the history of special education, provide one or two descriptive statements on their contribution to special education. Also important in the understanding of the history of special education would be for you to make this list in order according to the date, to make note of the country/continent of origin, and to note from what discipline each person is represented: (p.18-20)

Itard	Gallaudet	Seguin
Montessori	Howe	Pinel

6. What are the three major functions of parent organizations? (p.20,21)

7. Name three laws that have had a major impact on special education in the United States. After naming each law, provide one or two statements describing each law's major intent. (p.22,23)

B. Understanding The Facts

8. What is the difference between a disability and a handicap? (p.6)

9. Determining the prevalence of exceptional children would seem to be an easy task. Why is this *not* the case? (p.7)

10. One of the goals of early intervention programs is to reduce the chances of *at-risk* children requiring extensive special education services. In spite of the fact that this objective is being met, the number of children with special learning needs is increasing. Why? (p.23,24)

11. Provide a rationale for early intervention programs for exceptional children. (p.31,32)

C. Applying The Facts

12. John is an identified behavior disordered student placed in a regular classroom. His referral form indicates that high stress situations lead to anti-social behavior. At this early stage of his integration, John is left in the regular class without assistance from the behavioral resource teacher. Would the environment be characterized as *handicapping* or *disabling* for this child? Justify your response. (p.6)

13. Mary has a specific learning disability in reading. The resource teacher has recommended one-to-one instruction for one hour every day. Mary's parents, however, want Mary placed in a self-contained classroom in order to get the special attention they feel she needs (Mary is progressing satisfactorily in all other subject areas). Mary's parents claim that the law entitles Mary to placement in a special class. Should Mary's parents get what they want? Why or why not? (p.24-26)

14. Jeffrey needs resource help every day for reading and spelling. The school does not have a special program. The principal has offered to hire a special teacher for Jeffrey if Jeffrey's parents will pay the teacher's salary. The parents do not feel that they should do this? Are the parents correct? Will Jeffrey receive service? (p.23-25)

15. Michel has been referred for special education testing because he cannot read. Michel's family, who speak only French at home, has only lived in the U.S. for eight months. Michel's father requests that Michel be tested in French. The psychologist, however, says that testing must be done in English. What should be the final decision? Why? (p.25)

16. The Riverside School System has been refusing to assess any new students that are being referred for special education services. The administration office says that their school system has over-extended their budget and depleted any funds that could be used to serve the handicapped. Can the administration do this? Why or why not? (p.22-24)

FILL-IN-THE-BLANKS

Fill in the number of the most appropriate term listed under <u>Terms To Note</u> for each of the following statements.

1. For Marilyn, who is visually impaired, the ___ is the regular classroom. Steven, however, displays severe behavior disorders and is more appropriately placed in a self-contained classroom.

2. The process of providing a learning and living environment that is as similar to that of most individuals is otherwise known as ___.

3. Mr. Bright, who was a painter, lost the use of his right arm. Since his accident, he has become a radio announcer. Mr. Bright has a(n) ___.

4. The local courthouse is not accessible to physically handicapped individuals. This situation is a violation of ___.

5. Mr. Speedy, who is a long-distance runner, has been diagnosed as having Muscular Dystrophy. Mr. Speedy, who would like to continue running marathons, now has a(n) ___.

6. The role of ___ is to provide instruction that is specifically designed to meet the needs of exceptional children.

7. All teachers need to pay attention to ____ when using assessment tools.

8. It has been determined that in 1980, 95% of all weddings performed in Marry-In-A-Minute, USA, terminated in divorce. This statistic is a(n) ___ figure.

9. For a number of years in our state, the law that governed the use of seat belts was ___. Recently, however, the law to 'buckle up' has become ___.

10. A(n) ___ is a written agreement between the school and the home indicating the child's needs and what will be done to address those needs.

11. Making provisions for the young child in the home and in the classroom is essential in a(n) ___ program.

12. Special education services for exceptional children aged three-five is provided for in _____, and not in _____.

13. Preparing an individual for continuing education, future employment, and for a fulfilling lifestyle are all elements of a process called ___.

14. ___ require special education services and related services in order to reach their full potential.

15. Providing exceptional children with school experiences in the company of nonexceptional students is referred to as ___.

16. The rights of the parents of exceptional children are protected through ___. This includes rights to information, informed consent, and impartial hearings if a disagreement arises.

RETURN TO CHAPTER SUMMARY

Reread the chapter summary in the textbook (p.35-37) for a review of the facts, concepts, and issues presented in this introductory chapter.

ENRICHMENT ACTIVITIES

For your interest and further study...

1. Collect a listing of parent and/or professional organizations for the area of special education in which you would be interested to teach. Attend a local meeting of one of these organizations. Determine the role that this group played in advocating for state and federal legislation designed to meet the needs of exceptional children. What are the current functions of this organization?

2. Determine whether there is a Student Council for Exceptional Children (C.E.C.) in your university or college. Attend a social or professional meeting of this organization, and, through conversation with its members, determine the role and function of this organization.

3. Visit a Montessori school in your community. Compare your observations to what you have learned from your reading and class discussions.

C H A P T E R

2

Issues and Trends: Normalization, Integration, and Cultural Diversity

CHAPTER FOCUS

Many changes have taken place in the field of special education throughout the years. Chapter two highlights some of these changes by examining the principle of normalization. Issues and concerns such as labeling, disability rights, newborns with disabilities, technology, and media representation are all facets of the normalization process and are discussed within this chapter. Deinstitutionalization, another current trend, involves the placement of institutionalized individuals in appropriate settings within their communities. The purpose of this trend is to provide an environment that is as normal as possible. Mainstreaming has also been a trend in recent years. Although desirable, mainstreaming carries with it many ethical, moral, and research issues. Hallahan and Kauffman also address the complex issue of cultural diversity. Teachers must be aware of the dynamic nature of this issue, especially in assessment, instruction, and socialization initiatives.

CHAPTER OBJECTIVES

On completion of this chapter, the student should be able to discuss the following topics:

1. The principle of normalization
2. The advantages and disadvantages of labeling
3. The rights for which disabled individuals feel they need to fight

13

4. The complexity and implications of the issue of *quality of life* for newborns with disabilities
5. The role of technology in the process of normalization
6. The media's portrayal of the handicapped
7. The implications of deinstitutionalization
8. The principle of mainstreaming - both sides of the issue
9. Strategies for effective mainstreaming
10. The viewpoint of those who support the Regular Education Initiative
11. The complexity, dynamics, and implications of the diverse cultures that are represented within our educational system

TERMINOLOGY

Terms to Note:

The following terms are important to note. These terms will be used in a Fill-In-The-Blank exercise at the conclusion of this chapter.

1. normalization (p.40)
2. label (p.40)
3. handicapism (p.44)
4. integration (p.53)
5. deinstitutionalization (p.53-54)
6. Community Residential Facility (CRF) (p.54)
7. mainstreaming (p.56,57)
8. effective teaching research (p.58)
9. teacher consultant (p.59)
10. reverse mainstreaming (p.59)
11. prereferral teams (p.60)
12. cooperative learning (p.61)
13. peer tutoring (p.62)
14. regular education initiative (REI) (p.62,63)
15. cultural diversity (p.65,66)

MULTIPLE CHOICE

Select the most appropriate response.

A. Remembering The Facts

1. The principle of normalization states that: (p.40)

    a. all individuals, regardless of disability or cultural origin, should be viewed as normal by society.
    b. all disabled individuals should live and be educated in an environment that is as normal as possible - making the necessary modifications for the disability.
    c. all disabled individuals will become normal by being allowed to function as a normal person.
    d. all disabled individuals should live and be educated along with normal people with little or no adjustments for the disability.

2. Which of the following is seen as a problem in labeling children by their exceptionalities? (p.40,41)

    a. Labels can effect self-esteem.
    b. The label often becomes the person.
    c. Labels can increase discrimination.
    d. All of these are problems with labeling.

3. An advantage of labeling is that: (p.42,43)

    a. it assists with communication about an individual.
    b. it ensures that money for special education programs be provided.
    c. both a and b
    d. There are no advantages to labeling.

4. Institutions have become less popular in recent years because: (p.53,54)

    a. many have been found to be very inadequate and dehumanizing.
    b. research indicates that there is a decrease in cognitive and social competencies in many institutionalized individuals.
    c. many institutions fail to provide an atmosphere that is as *normal* as possible.
    d. both a and b
    e. all of the above

5. Which of the following statements is TRUE regarding residential facilities such as CRF's? (p.54,55)

    a. A large number of residents in residential facility will usually result in better care.
    b. Residential facilities were replaced by institutions in the 1960's.
    c. Residential facilities could provide a normal home-like environment.
    d. Residential facilities such as group homes and CRF's are more readily accepted into neighborhoods than are institutions accepted by the community or state/province.

6. In general, the efficacy studies (1950-1980) suggested that: (p.57)

    a. regular class placement resulted in increased social development.
    b. regular class placement resulted in decreased social development.
    c. special class placement resulted in lowered academic achievement.
    d. both b and c
    e. both a and b

7. In which of the following ways are teacher consultants similar to prereferral teams? (p.59,60)

    a. Both assist the general education teacher with students in the regular classroom.
    b. Both assist the resource room staff with students who have been referred for special education.
    c. Both actively work with small groups of students.
    d. Both are comprised of special education teachers.

8. The major goal of prereferral teams is: (p.60,61)

    a. to encourage parental involvement in the child's education.
    b. to reduce the number of unnecessary referrals to special education.
    c. to recommend more appropriate placements for students who are difficult to teach.
    d. to provide materials that will assist the classroom teacher in changing attitudes toward exceptional learners.

16

9. According to Slavin's studies in cooperative learning, in order for academic achievement to be enhanced, what must be present? (p.61,62)

    a. group incentives
    b. more nonexceptional students than exceptional students in the group
    c. individual accountability
    d. both a and c
    e. all of the above

10. The goal of the REI is to: (p.63)

    a. reduce the number of special education teachers.
    b. conduct research on effective teaching in the regular classroom.
    c. eliminate the need for special education.
    d. place the responsibility of educating exceptional learners on the regular education system.

11. The major goal of a multicultural educational system is to: (p.66)

    a. assist students in the development of a positive understanding and appreciation of their own culture.
    b. promote an understanding and appreciation of the various microcultures within the common culture.
    c. promote positive attitudes toward all cultures.
    d. both b and c
    e. all of the above

12. Which of the following types of tests provides useful information to teachers and can, in fact, reduce the cultural bias often associated with assessment? (p.70)

    a. standardized intelligence tests
    b. curriculum based tests
    c. standardized achievement tests
    d. both a and c
    e. both a and b

B. Understanding The Facts

13. Which of the following individuals would be most adversely affected by an institutional environment? (p.54)

    a. a child who was not receiving adequate physical or emotional care at home
    b. a child whose *school life* was inconsistent with his/her *home life*
    c. a child who has a healthy home/school environment
    d. all children are adversely affected by an institutional environment

14. Within the past decade, the major argument in favor of mainstreaming has been focused on ___. (p.56,57)

    a. academic issues
    b. ethical issues
    c. social issues
    d. teaching methodology

15. According to researchers such as Chalfont, Pysh, Moultrie, Gerber, and Semmel, which of the following may be the *expert* when a sixth grade teacher is encountering difficulties with an unruly group of adolescents? (p.61)

    a. a teacher consultant
    b. the principal
    c. another sixth grade teacher
    d. a parent group
    e. a psychologist

C. Applying The Facts

16. Which of the following statements best describes the principle of normalization and the least restrictive environment? (p.40)

    a. A moderately retarded teenager, who is unpredictably violent, is socially integrated into a primary physical education class. He has the assistance of a high school cooperative education student.
    b. A 16 year old moderately retarded girl is placed in a high school English class.
    c. A multihandicapped moderately retarded eight year old boy joins a second grade class for participation in a Peabody Language Lesson for three mornings per week.
    d. Walking into a specialized setting for moderately retarded teenagers, one hears the music of Mother Goose, Sesame Street, and the Chipmunks.

TRUE AND FALSE

Indicate whether the following statements are True or False. In your notebook, rewrite the False statements so that they are accurate.

1. Labeling exceptional individuals has advantages and disadvantages and therefore should be discontinued. (p.40,41)   T   F

2. Labeling assures *appropriate* services. (p.43)   T   F

3. Expectations and perceptions of disabled individuals can be biased by labels. (p.41,42)   T   F

4. If a specific technological advance allows a disabled individual to accomplish something otherwise impossible, it should be encouraged and attempted. (p.48)   T   F

5. Institutions that provide a *non-institutional* environment are more likely to be beneficial to exceptional individuals. (p.54)   T   F

6. There is much research to support the effectiveness of prereferral teams. (p.61)   T   F

7. There are many reports from teachers and administrators supporting the effectiveness of prereferral teams. (p.61)   T   F

8. Research indicates that cooperative learning can lead to attitude change, however, it does not necessarily affect academic achievement. (p.61)   T   F

9. Developing a positive attitude toward cultural groups different from one's own occurs *naturally* in most individuals. (p.66)   T   F

10. An exceptional individual could be identified *exceptional* in one ethnic group but not in another. (p.66,67)   T   F

11. Due to the possibility of *unfairness*, educational assessment can be misleading and is, therefore, damaging and unnecessary. (p.69,70)   T   F

SHORT ANSWER QUESTIONS

Answer the following questions in your notebook.

A. Remembering The Facts

1. What were the reasons supporting the antilabeling movement? How are these reasons justified? (p.40)

2. What are the five reasons for continued use of labels? (p.43)

3. Compare and contrast past civil rights movements with the current disability rights movement. (p.44)

4. Summarize the most recent research on Community Residential Facilities (CRF). (p.54,55)

5. List and discuss six of the most common strategies for effective implementation of mainstreaming. (p.58)

6. List eight characteristics of *effective teaching* according to Rosenshine's research. (p.58)

7. What is the role of a teacher consultant? Briefly list the 11 advantages of this service to teachers. (p.60)

B. Understanding The Facts

8. Explain how the concept of least restrictive environment relates to: a) normalization; b) deinstitutionalization; and c) mainstreaming. (p.11,12,40,53,56-58)

9. Technology has made a major impact on normalization efforts. How can technology be both a blessing and a curse for a handicapped individual? (p.48)

10. According to the authors, what was the major problem with the research that investigated the effectiveness of special classes for students with mild disabilities? (p.56,57)

11. Why might regular classroom teachers *not* support mainstreaming? (p.56-58)

12. How could the Effective Teaching Research be of assistance to teachers and administrators? (p.58,59)

13. What benefits may result from reverse mainstreaming? (p.59,60)

14. What is the difference between integration and mainstreaming? (p.53,56-58)

15. In addition to the examples given in the text, provide two alternate examples of how an exceptional student in an Anglo-dominant microculture may *not* be identified as exceptional in another microculture. (p.66,67)

16. Why is it important to differentiate between ethnicity and exceptionality? (p.67)

17. Briefly describe curriculum-based assessment. How does it address the problem of cultural diversity within North American classrooms?

C. Applying The Facts

18. One of the reasons for continuing with the practice of labeling exceptional children states that labeling can actually facilitate feelings of *tolerance*. How can a label help a nondisabled individual feel more tolerant of a disabled individual? How can a label help a disabled individual feel more tolerant of him/herself? (p.40-42)

FILL-IN-THE-BLANKS

Fill in the number of the most appropriate term listed under Terms to Note for each of the following statements.

1. ___ suggests that many low achieving students improve academically when the teaching methodology includes structure, a fast pace, clear instructions, many examples, and mastery.

2. Principal Barnes, in observing Mr. Jackson's fifth grade class, noticed that when the content of the lesson appeared to become increasingly difficult for some students, Mr. Jackson stopped instruction after some examples. He then sat down and allowed the more capable students to pair with those students who were having difficulty, in order to work together on another example. Subsequent to this lesson, Mr. Jackson explained to Principal Barnes that he was using ___.

3. At the conclusion of an IEP meeting, a(n) ___ was suggested for a youngster. This process resulted in funds being directed to provide special education service for this child.

4. A non-competitive, dynamic, and differentiated method of teaching and learning is known as ___.

5. Carl, who is severely mentally retarded, has left the state residential school and is now living with other disabled adults in a neighborhood home. Carl is a resident of a(n) ___ .

6. A group of five severely mentally retarded children are removed from a special school and placed in a specialized classroom within a community school. This is a(n) ___ attempt.

7. A superintendent directs a memo to all principals within the school district: "Beginning next term all special education settings will be eliminated. We are going to attempt to implement the suggestions put forth by those who support the ___ ."

8. Mr. Cole, who teaches in a self-contained classroom for intellectually handicapped adolescents, has a reputation of having the 'best' social skills program in the district. Ms. Matheson, a colleague of Mr. Cole, has a student who is in need of more intense social skills training than she can provide in the regular class. At lunch, these teachers discuss how the student could benefit from Mr. Cole's program. This is an example of an attempt at ___ .

9. Because the term ___ is a parallel of racism, a lowered status and inequality of experience for disabled individuals is implied.

10. Michelle is experiencing increasing difficulty with academic tasks related to mathematics in the regular class. Her teacher is experiencing increasing difficulty in keeping Michelle within the large group for instruction in math. She also feels that to refer Mary for special education services at this point might be presumptuous. Mary's teacher could utilize the benefit of ___ .

11. Becky is severely multihandicapped and needs special assistance in eating. When she was younger, Becky was always fed before the rest of the family. Now, with the assistance of various family members, she is fed at the regular mealtime with her family. This process could be referred to as ___ .

12. After school, there is a conference in the fifth grade classroom. In attendance are two fifth grade teachers, a fourth grade teacher, and the resource teacher. They are brainstorming on management strategies that could be utilized by the fourth grade teacher, in order to become more effective with an unruly student. This group of teachers could also be called a(n) ___ .

13. ___ refers to the transfer of disabled and/or handicapped individuals from large residential facilities to facilities in their local communities.

14. Because of the ___ of North America, it is imperative that educators provide appropriate assessment and education for all ethnic groups.

15. Vincent is six years old and is educationally blind. He has no other exceptionalities. For first grade, he will be spending the majority of his school day in the regular classroom, in addition to receiving specialized instruction from the local itinerant teacher for the visually impaired. This is an attempt at normalization and is known as ___.

RETURN TO CHAPTER SUMMARY

Reread the chapter summary in the textbook (p.74,75) for a review of the facts, concepts, issues presented in Chapter Two.

ENRICHMENT ACTIVITIES

For your interest and further study...

1. Throughout this course, note and record any incidents of handicapism that you observe at home, at school, at work, and/or within society. Also note and record your personal reaction to the incident.

2. Interview a regular classroom teacher, a special education teacher, and an administrator in order to compare and contrast various viewpoints on mainstreaming, integration, and the REI.

3. Visit a large urban school and discuss with the principal how the diversity of cultures represented in his/her school is addressed in terms of curriculum and instruction.

3

Mental Retardation

CHAPTER FOCUS

This chapter provides an introduction to mental retardation. Current definitions, classification systems, and causes are reviewed. A discussion on the assessment process is then followed by current perspectives in effective educational programming for mentally retarded students.

CHAPTER OBJECTIVES

On completion of this chapter, the student should be able to discuss the following topics:

1. The differences/similarities between a mentally retarded individual and a nonretarded individual
2. Two classification systems for mental retardation
3. Causes of mild retardation
4. Causes of more severe retardation
5. The diagnosis of retardation through measurement techniques
6. Limitations of tests of intelligence and adaptive behavior
7. Cognitive and personality characteristics of mentally retarded individuals
8. Components of educational programming for mildly and moderately retarded students
9. Components of educational programming for severely and profoundly retarded students
10. The basic tenets of applied behavior analysis
11. The most productive and appropriate educational placements for the various classifications of mental retardation

12. The significance of early intervention during the preschool years
13. Appropriate transition program options for retarded adults
14. Strategies to recommend to the general classroom teacher in order to facilitate effective instruction of mildly retarded students

TERMINOLOGY

<u>Terms To Note</u>:

The following terms are important to note. These terms will be used in a Fill-In-The-Blank exercise at the conclusion of this chapter.

1. mentally retarded (p.80)
2. adaptive behavior (p.80)
3. intellectual functioning (p.80)
4. mild retardation (p.81,82)
5. moderate retardation (p.81,82)
6. severe retardation (p.81,82)
7. profound retardation (p.81,82)
8. cultural-familial retardation (p.84)
9. Down syndrome (p.86)
10. Phenylketonuria (PKU) (p.89)
11. Tay-Sachs disease (p.89)
12. rubella (p.90)
13. meningitis (p.90)
14. encephalitis (p.90)
15. pediatric AIDS (p.90)
16. microcephalus (p.90)
17. hydrocephalus (p.90)
18. fetal alcohol syndrome (FAS) (p.91)
19. anoxia (p.92)
20. intelligence tests (p.92,93)
21. mental age (p.93)
22. tests of adaptive behavior (p.95)
23. metacognitive process (p.96,97)
24. readiness (p.102)
25. functional academics (p.102,103)
26. community-based instruction (p.103)
27. integrated therapy (p.103,104)
28. applied behavior analysis (p.104,105)
29. baseline (p.105)
30. community residential facility (p.106)
31. individualized transition plan (p.108)
32. sheltered workshop (p.111)
33. competitive employment (p.112)

MULTIPLE CHOICE

Select the most appropriate response.

A. Remembering the Facts

1. AAMR stands for D . (p.79,80)

    a. American Association on Mental Deficiency
    b. American Association for the Mentally Retarded
    c. American Association for Mild Retardation
    d. American Association on Mental Retardation

2. Which *two* characteristics must an individual exhibit during the developmental period in order to be classified as mentally retarded. (p.80)

    a. subaverage intellectual functioning and subaverage adaptive behavior
    b. subaverage intellectual functioning and subaverage language skills
    c. subaverage intellectual functioning and average adaptive behavior
    d. subaverage language skills and subaverage performance on a test of motor skills

3. The most useful classification system for mental retardation is the one proposed by the AAMR. This system uses the following terms: (p.81)

    a. educable, trainable, severe/profound
    b. subaverage, average, above average
    c. mild, moderate, severe, profound
    d. EMR, TMR, SPH

4. Karen scored 28 on a standardized test of intellectual functioning. On the basis of intellectual functioning alone, Karen would be classified as ___. (p.82)

    a. mildly retarded   c. severely retarded
    b. moderately retarded   d. profoundly retarded

5. Which of the following statements is FALSE regarding the lowered prevalence estimate of mental retardation in the late eighties? (p.83)

   a. Some children previously thought of as mentally retarded are now being labeled *learning disabled*.
   b. Advances in medical technology are resulting in fewer children born with cognitive deficits.
   c. In order for an individual to be classified as mentally retarded, he/she must exhibit a deficit in both cognitive functioning and adaptive behavior.
   d. In earlier years, there was a tendency to label minority children as mentally retarded.

6. Which of the following statements is FALSE concerning mild retardation? (p.83,84)

   a. Many mildly retarded individuals have cultural and familial retardation.
   b. Causes of mild retardation are, in most cases, similar to the causes of more severe retardation.
   c. Both heredity and environment can contribute to mild retardation.
   d. An individual with mild retardation is usually similar in appearance to a nonretarded individual.

7. The most commonly utilized standardized intelligence test(s) in the identification of mentally retarded children is/are ___. (p.92)

   a. The Stanford-Binet
   b. The Adaptive Behavior Scale
   c. The Wechsler Intelligence Scale for Children-Revised
   d. The Kauffman Assessment Battery for Children
   e. both a and c
   f. both a and d

8. The most commonly utilized test(s) of adaptive behavior in the identification of mentally retarded children is/are___. (p.95)

   a. The AAMD Adaptive Behavior Scale-School Edition
   b. The Adaptive Behavior Inventory for Children
   c. The Social Competency Scale for Children and Adults
   d. both a and b
   e. both a and c

27

9. Which of the following would NOT be evaluated on a test of adaptive behavior? (p.95)

a. personal hygiene skills
b. managing money
c. social etiquette
d. spelling skills
e. cooperation with others

10. The most obvious characteristic of an individual with mental retardation is ___. (p.95)

a. a physical characteristic
b. emotional instability
c. a reduced ability to learn
d. the inability to become independent
e. all of the above

11. Which of the following is an essential component of an educational program for severely/profoundly retarded students? (p.103)

a. learning to read a telephone book
b. learning through participation in functional activities
c. learning how to complete a job application
d. learning to discriminate between various numbers and letters

12. In the application of applied behavior analysis, a baseline is essential because: (p.105)

a. it specifies the next instructional objective.
b. it provides information on the current level of knowledge or functioning.
c. it provides the basis for comparison to later learning.
d. both b and c
e. all of the above

13. Into which type of special education service are mildly retarded students most likely placed? (p.106)

a. regular classroom
b. regular classroom with resource assistance
c. special classroom with social integration
d. special day school
e. residential school

28

B. Understanding the Facts

14. Which of the following statements is TRUE? (p.78,79)

    a. A retarded child is more similar to a nonretarded child than he/she is different.
    b. It is very easy to 'pick out' a mentally retarded child.
    c. Children with mental retardation go through very different stages than nonretarded children.
    d. Most retarded children grow up to become very dependent adults.

15. Beth has scored 65 on the WISC-R and performs poorly on academic tasks. She has adequate communication skills, good *common sense*, and is very independent. Beth could be classified as ___. (p.80-82)

    a. learning disabled
    b. mentally retarded
    c. academically disabled
    d. an average student
    e. none of the above

16. Randy is unable to handle responsibilities that are normally assumed by twelve year olds. At recess, he can often be found playing with the kindergarten students. On a recent IQ test, Randy scored 68. Randy would most likely be classified as ___. (p.80-82)

    a. learning disabled
    b. mentally retarded
    c. socially disabled
    d. an average student
    e. none of the above

17. Adaptive behavior can be defined as: (p.80)

    a. the ability to develop and maintain appropriate social interactions in school.
    b. the degree to which an individual can meet age-related standards of independence and social responsibility.
    c. the degree to which an individual can adapt to the environment with the assistance of adaptive devices.
    d. the degree to which an individual can adapt and adjust during the postsecondary school years.

18. Danny's IQ test resulted in a score of 54. Which of the following 'labels' would NOT accurately describe Danny? (p.81,82)

    a. severely retarded   c. mildly retarded
    b. moderately retarded   d. educable mentally retarded

19. The authors state reasons why there is a discrepancy between past and present prevalence estimates for mental retardation. All of these reasons are most reflective of which classification of mental retardation? (p.83)

a. mild
b. moderate
c. severe
d. profound

20. Mild retardation would most likely be suspected at: (p.83)

a. birth, by the attending physician or obstetrician.
b. home, by the parent(s) during the preschool years.
c. school, by the teacher(s).
d. work, by the supervisor or employer.

21. If adaptive behavior was NOT a criteria in determining mental retardation: (p.83)

a. we would have fewer 'six-hour retarded children'.
b. prevalence estimates for mental retardation would increase.
c. there would be fewer minority and low socioeconomic level children identified as mentally retarded.
d. prevalence estimates would remain unchanged.

22. Which of the following statements reflect our current research-based understanding of the *Nature vs. Nurture Controversy*? (p.84-86)

a. Environment has been cited as the most influential determinant of intelligence.
b. Heredity has been cited as the most influential determinant of intelligence.
c. Both heredity and environment contribute to intelligence, however, the exact contribution of each is not easily determined.
d. The contribution of both heredity and environment can be determined in many cases.

23. An IQ test indicates that a seven year old child has a mental age of 4-2. This implies that: (p.93)

a. the child performed on this particular test in a similar fashion as an average child with a chronological age of 4-2.
b. the child can be compared to other children who have a chronological age of 4-2.
c. this child should be placed in a preschool setting.
d. this child thinks in the same way as an average child of age 4-2 thinks.

24. The *primary goal* of preschool programs for children who are at-risk for developing mild retardation is: (p.107)

    a. reducing the probability that these children will be identified and classified as retarded when they enter school.
    b. to help these children achieve their highest possible cognitive and social level.
    c. to improve parenting techniques at home.
    d. to assist parents in providing the best nutrition and health care.

C. Applying the Facts

25. Danielle is a 11 year old severely/profoundly retarded student. She needs to learn how to zip and unzip her jacket. The most effective method of teaching Danielle this skill is to: (p.103)

    a. use her own jacket and teach/practice the skill on every occasion in which the jacket is used.
    b. use her own jacket and teach/practice the skill at a specific time (10:00 a.m.) each day.
    c. practice with a similar jacket on a doll each day.
    d. use a large zipper (no jacket attached) on which to practice each day.

26. Linda, age 15, is mildly retarded. She is experiencing increasing difficulty in managing mathematics within the regular classroom. She is now at least two grade levels behind her peers. The most important advice to provide for Linda's teacher would be: (p.102)

    a. to excuse Linda from math class from now on.
    b. to teach Linda only those mathematical skills that will assist in her independence as an adult.
    c. to enlist a resource teacher's assistance or encourage her parents to hire a tutor to help her to 'catch up and keep up' with her peers.
    d. put Linda back one or two grades.
    e. both c and d

27. Heather is multihandicapped (including severe retardation). Her educational program includes speech and physical therapy. The most effective approach in teaching Heather the generalization of correct speech sounds and appropriate language skills is to: (p.103,104)

    a. have Heather see a speech/language therapist each day.
    b. have Heather receive intense speech/language therapy
       from her teacher at a specific time each day.
    c. have Heather practice correct speech sounds and
       appropriate language skills in every situation
       throughout the day in which speech/language is
       required.
    d. have Heather practice appropriate speech and language
       skills at home.
    e. both c and d

28. Jonathan is classified as moderately retarded. He has been unable to master functional reading and mathematical skills. He is a very happy and sociable young man who excels in sports.   Which of the following administrative arrangements would be appropriate and productive for Jonathan? (p.106)

    a. regular classroom with resource assistance in
       reading and math
    b. special class placement with social integration with
       peers
    c. special class placement with integration in
       nonacademic subject areas such as music and physical
       education
    d. residential placement
    e. either a or b
    f. both b and c

TRUE AND FALSE

Indicate whether the following statements are True or False. In your notebook, rewrite the False statements so that they are accurate.

1. The level of cognitive functioning in a mentally retarded individual remains quite stable throughout his/her lifetime. (p.79,80)   T   F

2. Mental retardation is diagnosed on the basis of an IQ score. (p.80)   T   F

3. A commonly used standardized test of intellectual functioning is the Wechsler Intelligence Scale for Children-Revised. (p.80)   T   F

4. The most useful classification system for mental retardation is the system proposed by the AAMR. (p.81)
(T)   F

5. Being labeled *learning disabled* is more socially acceptable than being labeled *mentally retarded*. (p.83)
(T)   F

6. The only reason why prevalence estimates for mental retardation are decreasing is because of the utilization of more sophisticated assessment procedures. (p.83)   T   (F)

7. Most individuals who have been identified as mentally retarded are classified as *mildly* retarded. (p.83) (T)   F

8. The classic Skeels and Dye study of 1939 provided substantial support for the *nature* position in the Nature vs. Nurture controversy. (p.84,85)   T   (F)

9. Both intelligence and adaptive behavior can be measured using similar instruments and techniques. (p.92,95)
T   (F)

10. Intelligence tests are helpful in making placement decisions, however, they are not exempt from error in determining how an individual will function in the real world. (p.92,93)   (T)   F

11. Recent research concerning employment of retarded adults has indicated that job responsibility and social competence are better predictors of job success than is task production. (p.111)   (T)   F

MATCHING

I. Match the following *Genetic Factors* with its description. (p.86-89)

a. Down syndrome
b. phenylketonuria
c. Tay-Sachs disease
d. mosaicism
e. translocation
f. trisomy 21

1. _d_   is a type of Down syndrome in which some of the body cells have an extra chromosome and others do not.
2. _a_   is a condition resulting from chromosonal abnormalities that can be identified by specific physical characteristics such as hypotonia, slightly slanted eyes, and small oral cavity.
3. _c_   is a progressive disease which occurs primarily among those of East European origin.
4. _f_   is the most common type of Down syndrome.

5. _B_ results in abnormal brain development and can be controlled by a special diet.
6. _e_ is a type of Down syndrome in which the extra chromosome of the twenty-first pair becomes attached to another chromosome pair.

II. Match each of the following conditions that results in *Brain Damage* to its description. (p.90-92)

a. rubella
b. herpes simplex
c. syphilis
d. meningitis
e. encephalitis
f. anoxia

g. pediatric AIDS
h. microcephalus
i. hydrocephalus
j. fetal alcohol syndrome
k. teratogens

1. _h_ is a condition identified by a small conical skull.

2. _k_ is another term for substances that can cause abnormal fetal development.

3. _a_ in the mother during the first trimester of pregnancy is the most dangerous to the developing child.

4. _d_ can occur after birth when a child comes in contact with a bacteria/virus.

5. _i_ results from an overproduction of cerebrospinal fluid and can be identified by an enlarged skull.

6. _b_ or ____ acquired during the final phase of pregnancy stages a great risk for abnormal brain development.

7. _e_ results in more extensive brain damage than is caused by meningitis.

8. _j_ can be completely preventable if a pregnant woman abstains from alcoholic beverages during pregnancy.

9. _a_ is predicted to become the leading cause of mental retardation and brain damage.

10. _f_ is a term that refers to a deprivation of oxygen.

SHORT ANSWER QUESTIONS

Answer the following questions in your notebook.

A. Remembering the Facts

1. Identify the three critical elements of the definition of mental retardation. (p.80)

2. What are the three reasons for the most recent prevalence estimates for mental retardation being *lower* than earlier prevalence estimates? p.(83)

3. Briefly describe the Nature vs. Nurture controversy. What were the significant conclusions of both the 1939 study (Skeels and Dye) and the 1989 study (Capron and Duyme)? (p.84-86)

4. Identify and briefly describe the two main causes of severe cases of retardation. (p.86-92)

5. List four reasons why caution must be exercised in the use of intelligence tests. (p.92-95)

6. Identify and briefly describe four specific cognitive characteristics of mentally retarded individuals. (p.95-97)

7. Explain the difference in the *goals* of preschool programs for mildly retarded and/or at-risk children and preschool programs for moderately and/or severely retarded children. (p.107,108)

8. Describe the components of an effective individualized transition plan. (p.108)

B. **Understanding the Facts**

9. What is the significance of including the element of *adaptive behavior* in the definition of mental retardation? (p.80)

10. Why is the AAMR's classification system for mental retardation more *useful* than the Educator's classification system? (p.81,82)

11. What are the benefits of employing peer tutors to assist with the instruction of retarded students? Provide several guidelines that would assist a teacher in implementing such a program in his/her classroom. (p.104)

C. **Applying the Facts**

12. The authors have suggested four reasons why caution must be exercised when using intelligence tests. What might be some cautions associated with tests of adaptive behavior? (p.92-95)

13. Identify the four cognitive areas in which retarded individuals have difficulty (p.95-97). For each area, suggest a teaching strategy/technique or general teaching behavior that may assist retarded students in improving in these areas.

14. Suggest some ways in which the general classroom teacher can increase the social acceptance of a mildly retarded student. (p.98-99)

15. During a local meeting of the AAMR, a debate develops on the issue of age-appropriate curriculum and materials for severely/profoundly retarded individuals. Provide one or two arguments for each side of this issue. (p.103)

16. Consider the example of Keith, age 14, who is moderately retarded. Keith begins splashing water out of the sink as soon as he is to begin washing dishes. An applied behavior analysis approach is enforced. Provide the next five steps that would be consistent with this approach. (p.104,105)

17. Using the classification of mild, moderate, and severe/profound, indicate a)the most appropriate and productive educational placement - utilize the Special Education Services as outlined in Chapter One, 2)the type of curriculum that would be most appropriate and productive, and 3)the degree of integration that would be the most appropriate and productive. (p.106)

18. Write a 'memo' to your school administrator suggesting the implementation of reverse mainstreaming within your school. Provide a rationale for this technique as well as implementation suggestions. (p.59,60,116,117)

19. This chapter has provided many practical suggestions for the instruction of mildly retarded students. Construct five statements that would reflect some of the important considerations you have learned throughout this chapter. How will these statements guide your planning should a mildly retarded student be placed within your classroom?

FILL-IN-THE-BLANKS

Fill in the number of the most appropriate term listed under Terms To Note for each of the following statements.

1. Billy was diagnosed as having ___ at birth. His parents were instructed on how to control this condition through diet in order to prevent brain damage.

2. ___ is a significant cause of retardation that a pregnant woman, by consuming alcohol, can inflict upon her unborn child.

3. A(n) ___ approach to teaching, which is based on learning theory, is very effective for the instruction of retarded students with severe learning problems.

4. Nancy has very inadequate adaptive behavior in addition to an IQ score of 29. David is showing an improvement in adaptive behavior and scored 67 on his most recent IQ assessment. According to the AAMR classification system, Nancy would be classified as having ___, whereas David would be classified as having ___.

5. A question such as: "How does your child respond to guests coming into your home for dinner?" would be an example of an item on a(n) ____.

6. Incidence of ___ occurs predominantly among Achkenazi Jews and results in premature death.

7. The teacher is attempting to teach Marcy, who has mild retardation, to use the strategy of clustering in an attempt to learn important phone numbers. Marcy is learning a(n) ___.

8. Another name for a group home is a(n) ___.

9. Adequate and appropriate communication skills, social skills, and self-help skills are all components of ___.

10. Ms. Maxwell determines that Robby has difficulty playing independently during free time. Her accurate record-keeping indicates that Robby will 'float' around the classroom for an average of 11 minutes before settling into a productive activity. Ms. Maxwell has taken a(n) ___ measurement.

11. Joe is 19 years old and is moderately retarded. He is learning to read food labels, read the TV guide, and make correct change. Joe is benefiting from a(n) ___ program at his school.

12. Cara's mother and older brother have been identified as retarded. As soon as Cara started school, it was evident that she would need a great deal of extra teaching and assistance in order to keep up with her peers. Due to Cara's environment and genetic history, Cara will most likely exhibit characteristics of retardation. The cause of this type of retardation is often referred to as ___.

13. ___ is estimated to account for 10 percent of all moderate and severe cases of retardation. Because of the unique physical characteristics of this condition, it is fairly easy to identify.

14. A question such as: "What would be the thing to do if you found a ten dollar bill on the sidewalk by your school?" is an example of an item that may be on a(n) ____.

15. Self-help skills, following directions, auditory discrimination, language skills, and social skills are all components of a(n) ___ program.

16. Marianne's IQ test scores place her in a 'below average' range. Also, when compared to her peers, Marianne displays poor communication skills, inadequate social skills, and is very dependent on others for help with tasks associated with daily living. Marianne is ___.

17. A(n) ___ is a very structured nonintegrative environment created for mentally retarded adults who have relatively low skill development. ___ , on the other hand, provides less structure, better pay, and an opportunity to work with nondisabled individuals.

18. Infections during pregnancy can contribute to malformations of the cranial structure which can result in retardation. ___ is characterized by a very small head, whereas, ___ is identified by an enlarged head.

19. ___ is another name for German measles.

20. On an IQ test, Patricia, age 12, performed as well as an average nine year old. The IQ test results may indicate that Patricia has a(n) ___ of nine years, and therefore, an IQ score of 90.

21. Mr. James teaches in a self-contained classroom in which seven students have been placed. All of these students are very dependent on him and his two assistants. Intelligence testing has indicated that all of these students fall below the score of 25. According to the AAMR's classification system for mental retardation, Mr. James' students have ___. Mr. James is allowed a substantial budget for individual/class excursions outside of the classroom in order to teach his students the skills necessary for those settings. Mr. James is utilizing ___ in order to teach his students.

22. A(n) ___ can be incorporated into a retarded student's IEP and is very useful in attempting to create a smooth transition into adulthood.

23. ___ is determined on the basis of a standardized test of intelligence.

24. ___ is an infection of the covering of the brain. ___ is described as an inflammation of the brain. Both of these conditions can occur during infancy or childhood and can result in brain damage.

25. The problem of ___ occurs if, during the birth process, the child is deprived of oxygen.

26. According to the AAMR's classification system, an IQ score of 44 would indicate ___ .

27. ___ is a condition that is passed on to the unborn child during pregnancy. It is projected that this condition will become the leading cause of retardation and brain damage.

28. Shelly has cerebral palsy and moderate retardation. The professionals providing speech therapy and physical therapy bring their expertise into the classroom to assist Shelly and her teacher, rather than meeting Shelley in a therapy room for exercises. In this situation, ___ is being utilized.

RETURN TO CHAPTER SUMMARY

Reread the chapter summary in the textbook (p.118,119) for an effective review of the information presented on the topic of Mental Retardation.

ENRICHMENT ACTIVITIES

For your interest and further study...

1. Visit a local group home or CRF for mentally retarded adults during a recreational period. Observe the social and communication skills displayed by the residents.

2. Visit a sheltered workshop and/or a setting which provides competitive employment for mentally retarded adults.

3. Select an age/grade level at which you would be interested to teach. Visit a resource room for that level and inquire regarding the teaching strategies and materials that are utilized in the effective instruction of mildly retarded students. How do these methods and materials compare with those used in the regular classroom?

4

Learning Disabilities

CHAPTER FOCUS

It has been less than three decades since children with
learning disabilities have been identified as a separate
group of exceptional children. At the present time, this
group of children represents the largest group of
exceptional children being served in our school systems.
The number and diversity of children grouped under this
label has been attributed to the difficulty in defining the
precise nature of learning disabilities. In addition to
educational approaches and remediation strategies for these
students, this chapter presents the latest research on
causes, characteristics, and assessment of learning disabled
children.

CHAPTER OBJECTIVES

On completion of this chapter, the student should be able to
discuss the following topics:

1. What a learning disability IS and what it IS NOT
2. The reasons for confusion among professionals regarding
   definition
3. The possible causes for learning disabilities
4. Formal and informal methods of assessment that are used
   to diagnose learning disabilities
5. How the most common characteristics of learning disabled
   children interfere with the learning process
6. Educational methodologies that can be used with learning
   disabled children
7. The affective and social needs of learning disabled
   students

8. The unique problems of special populations, such as early childhood, adolescence, and adulthood
9. Strategies to suggest to general classroom teachers for effective instruction of learning disabled students

TERMINOLOGY

Terms To Note:

The following terms are important to note. These terms will be used in a Fill-In-The-Blank exercise at the conclusion of this chapter.

1. IQ-achievement discrepancy (p.124,125)
2. central nervous system dysfunction (p.125)
3. psychological processing disorder (p.125,126)
4. learning disabilities (p.126,127)
5. mixed dominance (p.128)
6. CT scan (p.128)
7. EEG (p.128)
8. process test (p.130)
9. informal reading inventory (p.131)
10. formative evaluation methods (p.131,132)
11. criterion-referenced testing (p.132)
12. curriculum-based assessment (p.132)
13. generalization (p.133)
14. maintenance (p.133)
15. attention-deficit hyperactivity disorder (p.135-137)
16. metacognition (p.137-139)
17. external locus of control (p.141)
18. attributions (p.141)
19. learned helplessness (p.141)
20. a learning disabled child (p.142)
21. process training (p.144)
22. structured program (p.145)
23. stimulus reduction (p.148)
24. cognitive training/cognitive behavior modification (p.150)
25. self-monitoring (p.151,152)
26. mnemonic keyword method (p.152)
27. self-instruction (p.153)
28. reciprocal teaching (p.153)
29. direct instruction (p.154)
30. preacademic skills (p.155)
31. functional academics (p.157)
32. work-study program (p.157)
33. learning strategies curriculum (p.157,158)

MULTIPLE CHOICE

Select the most appropriate response.

A. Remembering the Facts

1. Which of the following is NOT a problem with any learning disabled children? (p.122)

    a. hyperactivity
    b. low intelligence
    c. inattentiveness
    d. learning strategies
    e. academic problems in at least one skill area

2. Which of the following categories share some similar characteristics with learning disabilities? (p.122)

    a. emotionally disturbed   d. both a and b
    b. behavior disordered   e. all of the above
    c. mentally retarded

3. The individual instrumental in describing learning disabilities as a new category of special education was ___. (p.122)

    a. S. Engelmann   c. William Cruickshank
    b. Marianne Frostig   d. Samuel Kirk

4. In what way is the term *minimally brain injured* inadequate in describing a learning disabled child? (p.122,124)

    a. The term was educationally meaningless because
       it offered no intervention strategies.
    b. The term suggested that the brain was severely
       damaged.
    c. The term gave a connotation of hopelessness in
       attempting to implement an educational program.
    d. both a and c
    e. none of the above

5. During the 1987-88 year, the U.S. Department of Education reported that ___ of the school-age population was receiving services for learning disabilities. (p.127)

    a. .5 - 1%   d. 7 - 8%
    b. 2 - 3%   e. 10 - 15%
    c. 4 - 5%

6. Research by Engelmann and Lovitt has shown that poor academic achievement is often caused by ___.   (p.129)

    a. brain damage
    b. poor teaching
    c. processing disorders
    d. poor nutrition
    e. mixed dominance

7. Which of the following assessment instruments has its origins within the field of learning disabilities?   (p.130)

    a. standardized achievement tests
    b. process tests
    c. informal reading inventories
    d. formative evaluation methods

8. Which of the following assessment instruments attempts to measure visual perception? (p.130,131)

    a. DTVP
    b. KeyMath
    c. PIAT
    d. ITPA
    e. WISC-R

9. What is a disadvantage with informal reading inventories? (p.131)

    a. They are of little practical use.
    b. Suggested reading levels for students are too vague.
    c. They are very time-consuming.
    d. The reliability and validity of these tests depend upon the skill of the teacher.

10. Which of the following statements is TRUE?   (p.133)

    a. There are 99 characteristics that are typical of most learning disabled children.
    b. There are ten characteristics - in a variety of combinations - that are most frequently found in learning disabled children.
    c. Every learning disabled child needs only to exhibit one "LD" characteristic in order to be labeled.
    d. There are no typical characteristics of learning disabled children found in the literature.

11. Which of the following is NOT characteristic of the attention-deficit hyperactivity disorder? (p.135-137)

    a. inattention
    b. emotional lability
    c. impulsivity
    d. hyperactivity

12. Learning disabled children generally perform poorly on memory tasks because: (p.137)

    a. they are deficient in their use of strategies to help them recall material.
    b. they don't use any rehearsal strategies.
    c. they have poor phonological skills.
    d. both a and c
    e. both b and c

13. *Planning, evaluating, checking,* and *remediating* are all mechanisms involved in ___. (p.138)

    a. metacognition   d. attention
    b. impulsivity   e. locus of control
    c. memory

14. Which of the following would be LEAST useful as a source of evidence of social maladjustment? (p.138,140)

    a. parent ratings   d. medical records
    b. peer ratings   e. teacher ratings
    c. self-reports

15. Which of the following statements is FALSE concerning a learning disabled child? (p.142)

    a. He/she is an inactive learner.
    b. He/she is a passive learner.
    c. He/she lacks strategies for problem solving.
    d. He/she is unable to learn useful strategies for effective problem solving.
    e. He/she often lacks confidence in his/her learning abilities.

16. Most academic learning disabilities occur in the area of ___. (p.143)

    a. reading   d. writing
    b. spelling   e. mathematics
    c. oral communication

17. Current research on Cruickshank's stimulus reduction approach to teaching suggests that: (p.145,148)

    a. stimulus reduction guarantees academic progress.
    b. stimulus reduction leads to greater attending behavior.
    c. stimulus reduction assists in preparing a student for learning.
    d. both b and c
    e. all of the above

18. According to recent research, the most accurate predictors of later academic difficulties are tests of ___. (p.155)

   a. social maturity
   b. adaptive behavior
   c. psychological processes
   d. intelligence
   e. preacademic skills

19. The basic premise behind the Learning Strategies Curriculum is: (p.157,158)

   a. to assist learning disabled adolescents in learning strategies on how to learn.
   b. to assist learning disabled adolescents in learning specific subject content.
   c. to provide cognitive training for learning disabled adolescents.
   d. both a and c
   e. both b and c

B. Understanding the Facts

20. The controversy regarding the use of process training with learning disabled students is based on ___. (p.144,145)

   a. inadequate research
   b. ethical issues
   c. disagreements on the human development/maturation progression
   d. both a and b
   e. both b and c

21. A teacher teaches a small group of students by using a scripted lesson and hand signals. This teacher is using a ___ approach. (p.154)

   a. process training
   b. direct instruction
   c. multisensory
   d. behavior modification
   e. cognitive

C. Applying the Facts

22. Which of the following children would most likely be labeled *learning disabled*? (p.123,126,127)

   a. Donna, who is in seventh grade, scored 135 on a recent IQ test but reads at a fourth grade level.
   b. John, age 18, has not yet mastered basic reading and mathematics skills but is showing an improvement in his ability in the industrial arts curriculum.
   c. Jenny, who is in fifth grade, displays average performance on most academic tasks but has a tendency to engage in excessive fantasizing.
   d. Darryl is in third grade and scored 82 on a recent IQ test.

23. If you were responsible for assessment in your school system but had limited funds, which of the following assessment instruments or methods would be your best choice? (p.129-133)

   a. standardized tests
   b. process tests
   c. informal reading inventories
   d. formative evaluation methods

24. Marianne is able to read the words on the weekly spelling list when the words are printed in capital letters on the chalkboard. When reading them in her notebook, printed in lowercase letters, Marianne makes numerous errors. Marianne has difficulty with ___ . (p.133)

   a. hyperactivity
   b. generalization
   c. maintenance

   d. coordination
   e. spatial relations

MATCHING

Match each of the following educational approaches with the appropriate defining statements. (p.144-154)

a. Process Training
b. Multisensory approaches
c. Structure/Stimulus reduction
d. Medication

e. Cognitive training
f. Behavior modification
g. Direct instruction

1. _B_ suggests that children utilize as many of their senses as possible in learning new information
2. _G_ is a method of teaching in which the teacher takes the responsibility for ensuring that the student has acquired specific skills; the teacher focuses on the academic skills that the student needs to learn, rather than focusing on the underlying deficiencies in the student
3. _e_ stresses the importance of having the student take more responsibility for his/her own learning by teaching the student specific learning strategies
4. _A_ advocates 'training-the-deficit' and 'teaching through the preferred process'
5. _C_ assumes that learning disabled children with attentional problems and hyperactivity will be more productive in a structured atmosphere in which environmental stimulation is minimal
6. _f_ a method of systematically observing and recording the occurrence of specific events that precede and follow a targeted behavior for the purpose of changing that behavior
7. _D_ a controversial method of attempting to control characteristics such as attentional problems and hyperactivity

TRUE AND FALSE

Indicate whether the following statements are True or False. In your notebook, rewrite the False statements so that they are accurate.

1. Learning disabled children are less intelligent than their agemates and classmates. (p.122)   T   (F)

2. Learning disabilities, introduced in 1963, is the newest category of exceptionality. (p. 122)   (T)   F

3. The most commonly accepted definition of learning disabilities is the definition endorsed by the US federal government. (p.126)   (T)   F

4. In assessing learning disabilities, the most commonly used testing instrument is a teacher-made test. (p.129)   T   (F)

5. Recent research on Curriculum Based Assessment (CBA) suggests that this type of formative evaluation results in positive student progress. (p.132)   (T)   F

6. During the past three weeks Tom, age 11, has been talking excessively, interrupting occasionally, frequently losing his school books, spending a great deal of time out of his desk, and appears to be very restless.   Tom should be diagnosed as ADHD.   (p.135-137)   T   (F)

7. According to the literature, learning disabled children are most likely to possess an internal, rather than an external, locus of control. (p.141)   T   (F)

8. If there are no academic problems, a learning disability probably does not exist. (p. 142)   (T)   F

9. Research on perceptual-motor training has indicated that this approach is an effective method of assisting a learning disabled student improve reading skills.   (p.144,145)   T   (F)

10. Medication should never be used to treat hyperactivity. (p.148,149)   T   (F)

11. There are fewer programs and materials for learning disabled adolescents and adults because learning disabilities are usually *outgrown*. (p.156,157)   T   (F)

SHORT ANSWER QUESTIONS

Answer the following questions in your notebook.

A. Remembering the Facts

1. List four of the labels that had been used to describe the learning disabled population prior to 1963.   Why were these labels discarded? (p.122)

2. What are the five distinctions made between the Federal Definition and the NJCLD Definition of learning disabilities? (p.126,127)

3. List and briefly describe the three possible causes of learning disabilities.   (p.127-129)

4. Even though the ITPA does not 'measure up' as a valid testing instrument, it has brought about an important consideration in the assessment process.   What has been the ITPA's main contribution to the field of special education? (p.130,131)

5. Describe the five features of formative evaluation methods. (p.131,132)

6. Compare and contrast Criterion-Referenced Testing and Curriculum-Based Assessment. (p.132)

7. What four criteria MUST be met before a child can be diagnosed as ADHD? (p.136,137)

8. Why is cognitive training such a powerful tool for learning disabled students to possess? (p.150,151)

9. What are the issues regarding learning disabilities and early childhood education? (p.154,155)

10. List and briefly describe some of the options for programming for learning disabled students at the junior and senior high school level. (p.156-159)

11. Describe the characteristics of each transitional stage from high school to employment? What recommendations at each stage are suggested as being beneficial to a learning disabled young adult? (p.160)

B. Understanding the Facts

12. How is a child with learning disabilities different from a child with mental retardation? (p.80,122,126,127)

13. List the ten most common characteristics of learning disabilities. Provide one or two statements that would describe what each of these characteristics 'looks like' in a classroom situation. (p.133-144)

14. In a sentence, or by example, describe each of the five possible explanations for the socialization problems encountered by some learning disabled children. (p.140)

15. Explain the relationship that exists among *locus of control, attributions,* and *learned helplessness* as they pertain to learning disabled children. (p.141)

16. List the seven major educational approaches to learning disabilities. For each approach, provide a brief rationale, strengths/weaknesses of the approach, cautions (if any) in using the approach, and an example of what the approach would 'look like' in a classroom. (p.144-154)

17. How do *functional academics* and *learning strategies curriculum* differ? (p.157,159)

C. Applying the Facts

18. You are a resource teacher in your local school system. An administrator has just informed you that she is thinking of using the IQ-Achievement Discrepancy formula to determine which students are learning disabled. She asks for your opinion. Provide a rationale for NOT using this method of identification. What alternatives can you suggest? (p.124,125)

19. In 1985, the prevalence of learning disabilities in School System A was 21.3 percent. Now, in 1990, the prevalence estimate for learning disabilities is 15.7 percent. What factors could be responsible for this change? (p.127)

20. According to the data resulting from McKinney's Carolina Longitudinal Project, what caution must be exercised by educators with regard to the 'mainstreaming issue'? (p.134,135)

21. Consider the characteristics of a learning disabled individual. How could these characteristics decrease this person's 'employability' as an adult? Suggest some ways for a learning disabled adult to become more 'employable.' How can employers assist a learning disabled employee? (p.133-144,160,161)

22. Write a 'memo' to a college administrator concerning the lack of support provided to learning disabled students. What recommendations will you make? (p.160,161)

23. This chapter has provided many practical suggestions for general classroom teachers in the instruction of learning disabled students. Construct five statements that would reflect some of the important considerations that you have learned. How will these statements guide your planning should a learning disabled student be placed within your classroom?

FILL-IN-THE-BLANKS

Fill in the number of the most appropriate term listed under Terms To Note for each of the following statements.

1. Marg, who is a junior in college, *knows* that she needs to make extensive notes for herself, in addition to reading the assigned chapter before each class. She is demonstrating ___ skills.

2. The ___ approach to teaching learning disabled students focuses more on the instructional process that on the characteristics of the student.

3. ___ is a controversial factor that has been included within many definitions of learning disabilities.

4. Providing more and more responsibility to the students for their own learning is a component of the ___ technique of cognitive training.

5. *Talking myself through a task* would be a strategy in ___.

6. Reversing letters and numbers could be the result of a(n) ___.

7. When a student is assisted in becoming more aware and in control of his/her own attentional processes, he/she is said to be utilizing ___.

8. "Activity Centers! Activity Centers!" is all the rage. However, for some students, a(n) ___ is critical to student success.

9. Making up a budget, balancing a checkbook, and making change would all be topics in the mathematics component of a(n) ___ curriculum.

10. "I didn't study"; "It was a hard test"; "The teacher doesn't like me"; "I'm not good at math" are all negative ___ explaining why a student failed a math test. The specific statement, "The teacher doesn't like me" demonstrates a(n) ___. This type of belief system can lead to ___.

11. A(n) ___ can be determined through the use of a statistical formula.

12. A child who eats using the right hand and jumps by lifting off with the left foot could be said to have ___.

13. The ITPA is an example of a(n) ___.

14. A(n) ___ provides a picture of the brain, whereas, a(n) ___ provides a recording of the brain's activity.

15. Jason is very easily distracted by other children, noises, colors and lights in his regular classroom. In the resource room, however, he is less distracted because the resource room is carpeted, has no bulletin boards, and its windows are covered with blinds. The resource room teacher is utilizing ___ in order to assist Jason.

16. Carolyn, who has been identified as learning disabled, is a senior in secondary school. Part of her school day is spent in classes at school. The remainder of her day is spent at a Day-Care Center in order for her to learn job-related skills. Carolyn is involved in a(n) ____.

17. Among other factors, a child who does not actively involve him/herself in learning situations is called ___.

18. A(n) ___ could assist a teacher in determining at what point a student would become frustrated with reading material.

19. ___ is the *newest* category of special education.

20. The ___ addresses the three demands of a secondary school curriculum - acquiring information from written material, identifying and storing information, and demonstrating competence in written expression.

21. Standardized testing compares a student with his/her peers, whereas ___ compares a student with him/herself.

22. Kenny is learning to drive a car through his community's Driver Education Program. After his lesson, he experiences difficulty when he attempts to demonstrate his competence in his brother's car. Kenny is experiencing ___ difficulties.

23. ___ are those skills that are essential to be developed before more formal instruction can occur.

24. The ___ is an effective way of helping learning disabled students remember curriculum content, because it can make abstract information more concrete.

25. Mr. Jones determines that a student needs to master the following objective within a sequence of specific objectives: The student will understand the meaning of the prefix *dis-*. When mastery is reached, this student will be taught the next step in the sequence. Mr. Jones is using a formative evaluation method referred to as ___.

26. Self-questioning and ___ , both of which are components of cognitive training, assist the student by bringing a task under verbal control.

27. Laura studied cooking in her Home Studies program at school. During the fall semester, she learned how to make beef stew - she made it each week for the school cafeteria. Now, in the spring semester, she has been asked to make beef stew for a special luncheon for the staff at her school. Laura is anxious about this task because she has completely 'forgotten' how! She quickly enlists the assistance of her

former Home Studies teacher and requests some lessons. Laura is demonstrating some difficulties with ___.

28. Carol has been diagnosed as being learning disabled. She experiences a great deal of difficulty with auditory instructional methods. Consequently her teacher has Carol engage in many auditory training exercises. She also utilizes Carol's strength in visual processing as a basis for instruction. Carol's teacher is using a teaching methodology known as ___.

29. Ever since Kevin could walk, he has been extremely active and very easily distracted. Now, age 6, Kevin is in school and is demonstrating a great deal of 'out-of-seat' behaviors, difficulty waiting his turn, talking excessively - often without thinking, not finishing assigned tasks, and seems to be forever without a pencil! Kevin could be described as having ___.

30. Mr. Davidson's third grade students have been studying *geometry* in their mathematics class, and *magnets* in their science class. Therefore this week's spelling list includes words such as *triangle, sphere, cube, magnet, attract,* and *metal*. Mr. Davidson is using ___ in order to test his students' achievement.

RETURN TO CHAPTER SUMMARY

Reread the chapter summary in the textbook (p.167-169) for a helpful review of the information presented on the topic of Learning Disabilities.

ENRICHMENT ACTIVITIES

For your interest and further study...

1. Educational definitions for learning disabilities may vary from state to state. Obtain definitional statements from several states and compare them with how your own state defines learning disabilities.

2. Attend a meeting of a local parent group for learning disabled children. Take note of the issues and concerns that are discussed.

3. Interview two resource/special education teachers in your local school system. Determine which *treatment programs* (p. 144-154) are utilized most frequently. List materials that compliment the most prominent approaches.

C H A P T E R

5

Emotional/Behavioral Disorders

CHAPTER FOCUS

Problem behavior is becoming more prevalent in the school system. This chapter provides an overview of the possible causes and characteristics of children and youth who demonstrate emotional and behavioral disorders (E/BD). Educational approaches, interventions, and strategies are also explored.

CHAPTER OBJECTIVES

On completion of this chapter, the student should be able to discuss the following topics:

1. The factors that impact on the development of a universally accepted definition of E/BD
2. The current definition of E/BD that is generally agreed upon
3. Some classification systems for E/BD children
4. Prevalence of E/BD in children and youth
5. The factors that predispose and/or contribute to the development of E/BD
6. Identification and assessment of E/BD
7. The psychological and behavioral characteristics of E/BD children and youth, including children with psychotic disorders
8. The five conceptual models that guide educational practice regarding E/BD students
9. Appropriate educational placements for E/BD students, including those students with psychotic disorders
10. The factors that interfere with accurate early identification of E/BD

11. The unique challenges of an effective educational program for E/BD adolescents
12. Strategies to suggest to general classroom teachers for effective management and instruction of E/BD students

TERMINOLOGY

Terms To Note:

The following terms are important to note. These terms will be used in a Fill-In-The-Blank exercise at the conclusion of this chapter.

1. seriously emotionally disordered (p.173)
2. behaviorally disordered (p.173)
3. conduct disorder (p.178)
4. externalizing behavior (p.178,189,190)
5. internalizing behavior (p.178,191,192)
6. socialized aggression (p.178,190)
7. immaturity (p.178)
8. anxiety-withdrawal (p.178)
9. psychotic behavior (p.178)
10. motor excess (p.178)
11. autism (p.179,193)
12. schizophrenia (p.179,193)
13. predisposing factors (p.181)
14. contributing factors (p.181)
15. temperament (p.181)
16. sociopathic (p.190)
17. echolalia (p.194,195)
18. self-injurious behavior (p.195)
19. self-stimulation (p.195)
20. psychoanalytic approach (p.175,197,200)
21. psychoeducational approach (p.175,200)
22. humanistic approach (p.175,200)
23. ecological approach (p.172,175,200)
24. behavioral approach (p.175,201)
25. cognitive behavior modification (p.201)

MULTIPLE CHOICE

Select the most appropriate response.

A. Remembering the Facts

1. There are a number of reasons why so much difficulty has been encountered in arriving at a reliable definition of E/BD. Which of the following is NOT one of those reasons? (p.174-176)

    a. Disordered behavior is so subjective.
    b. There has not been enough research.
    c. Disordered behavior is culturally bound.
    d. There is an overlay among E/BD and other exceptionalities.

2. Tests designed to measure adaptive and maladaptive behavior are not generally accepted as the sole criteria for labeling a child E/BD because: (p.174,175)

    a. of the definitional problems associated with E/BD.
    b. there is no set criteria on *frequency* and *degree* of maladaptive behavior that would constitute E/BD.
    c. there are very few reliable and valid tests of this nature available.
    d. both a and b
    e. all of the above

3. Which of the following is an example of socialized aggression? (p.178)

    a. gang membership   c. hyperactivity
    b. hitting and biting   d. bizarre behavior

4. Which of the following is an example of a conduct disorder? (p.178)

    a. picking a fight with classmates
    b. obsessive/compulsive tendencies
    c. echolalic speech
    d. hyperactivity

5. Most recent prevalence estimates indicate that ___ of American schoolchildren are *identified* as seriously emotionally disturbed. (p.179,180)

    a. 1%   d. 5%
    b. 2%   e. 7%
    c. 3%

56

6. Which of the following types of problems are most prevalent in the E/BD population in schools? (p.180)

    a. internalizing   c. depression
    b. psychotic behavior   d. externalizing

7. Which of the following could be considered as a *contributing* factor in the development of E/BD? (p.181-184)

    a. family structure   d. school experiences
    b. temperament   e. both a and d
    c. cultural expectations f. all of the above

8. According to the most recent research on *family*, it is known that: (p.182)

    a. parental separation and divorce are very influential
       in the development of E/BD.
    b. an absent father is a prominent contributing factor
       in the development of E/BD.
    c. hostility within the family unit causes a child to
       become hostile and difficult to handle.
    d. the behavior of parents and children have reciprocal
       effects.
    e. parents are usually to blame for E/BD in children.

9. Which of the following statements is FALSE regarding the intelligence of E/BD students? (p.186)

    a. Many E/BD students score within the below average
       range.
    b. The majority of E/BD students score within the
       above average range.
    c. Some E/BD students score within the above average
       range.
    d. Some E/BD students score within the slow learner or
       mildly retarded category.

10. According to research on aggression, which of the following statements is FALSE: (p.191)

    a. Children can learn aggression from various models.
    b. The social learning theory is a helpful guide to
       aggression intervention.
    c. All types of *punishment* are ineffective and only
       produce counteraggression.
    d. Inconsistent and/or delayed aggressive punishment
       may actually increase aggression.

11. According to the authors, the three most important components of an educational program for most E/BD students are ___. (p.205)

  a. behavior modification, social skills training, and basic academics
  b. basic academics, social skills training, and affective education
  c. social skills training, moral education, and career counselling
  d. basic academics, career counselling, and affective education

B. Understanding the Facts

12. A reason why the term *seriously emotionally disturbed* has been replaced by terms such as *behavior disorders* or *emotionally/behaviorally disordered* is because: (p.172,173)

  a. it is the term used in federal legislation.
  b. it is more accepting by parents and peers.
  c. it is less stigmatizing and more accurate.
  d. both b and c
  e. all of the above

13. Which of the following statements is FALSE? (p.174,175)

  a. *Normal* behavior and *abnormal* behavior are two very different sets of behavior.
  b. The difference between *normal* behavior and *abnormal* behavior is usually one of degree, not kind.
  c. There is no distinct line between what is considered to be *normal* and that which is considered *abnormal*.
  d. There is a wide range of behavior that can be considered *normal*.

14. It could be assumed that the school could be a contributing factor in the development of behavioral difficulties because: (p.184)

  a. behavioral disorders are usually caused by traumas faced in a school situation.
  b. behavior disorders do not become obvious until at least age six or seven.
  c. many youngsters do not exhibit behavioral difficulties until after they enter school.
  d. many children just behave badly in the hours that they attend school.

15. Managing aggression, from a social learning perspective, involves which of the following techniques? (p.191)

   a. positive outcomes of nonaggressive, prosocial behavior.
   b. assisting youngsters in learning self-management through effective modeling and role-playing
   c. utilization of *time-out*
   d. both a and c
   e. all of the above

16. According to the social learning theory, which of the following interventions would most effectively assist a child who displays internalizing tendencies? (p.192)

   a. Encourage the child to talk about his/her feelings.
   b. Provide numerous opportunities to learn and practice appropriate responses.
   c. Provide counselling and medication.
   d. Provide rewards for appropriate and improved behavior.
   e. both a and b
   f. both b and d

C. Applying the Facts

17. Which of the following behaviors could be expected of a E/BD youngster AND a 'non-E/BD' youngster? (p.174,175)

   a. screaming   d. both a and b
   b. swearing   e. all of the above
   c. hitting/biting

18. Why is there a discrepancy between the prevalence estimate of E/BD and the number of children being served? (p.179,180)

   a. social policy   d. both a and b
   b. economic factors   e. both b and c
   c. unreliable measurement f. all of the above

19. According to current research on aggression, which of the following appears to be the most powerful factor in *cause* and *cure*? (p.191)

   a. genetic information   d. diet and hormones
   b. social learning   e. academic success
   c. temperament   f. both a and b

MATCHING

Match each of the following educational approaches with the correct description: (p.175,196-201)

a. psychoanalytical approach   d. ecological approach
b. psychoeducational approach   e. behavioral approach
c. humanistic approach

1. ____ advocates openness, freedom, innovation, self-direction, and self-evaluation; activities are more student-directed than teacher-directed
2. ____ suggests that misbehavior results from internal conflicts; intervention involves *uncovering* and *understanding* these conflicts
3. ____ proposes that it is the *interaction* of the child and the environment that causes behavioral difficulties; intervention involves home, school, and community
4. ____ suggests that all behavior is *learned*; intervention consists of rearranging antecedent events and consequences in order to learn new behaviors
5. ____ suggests a combination of psychiatric and educational concerns; intervention is directed at assisting the child in gaining *insight* into his/her behavior

TRUE AND FALSE

Indicate whether the following statements are True or False. In your notebook, rewrite the False statements so that they are accurate.

1. One of the most obvious problems of E/BD children is their inability to form close and satisfying relationships with others. (p.172)   T   F

2. There is no universally accepted definition of E/BD. (p.174)   T   F

3. A mentally healthy individual would never exhibit any characteristics of mental illness. (p.175)   T   F

4. There is an equal distribution of E/BD among males and females. (p.180)   T   F

5. Disordered behavior is not just a result of biological misfortune. (p.181-184)   T   F

6. *Modeling* appears to be instrumental in both learning and unlearning aggression. (p.191)   T   F

7. Internalizing behaviors would be viewed by a behaviorist as being caused by internal conflicts and an inadequate environment. (p.192)   T   F

8. Childhood and adulthood depression share similar characteristics. (p.192)   T   F

9. Children with severe E/BD appear similar to children with mental retardation and/or sensory impairments. (p.194)
T   F

10. Conceptual models of the approaches to E/BD are somewhat incompatible and, therefore, should seldom be combined. (p.196,197)   T   F

SHORT ANSWER QUESTIONS

Answer the following questions in your notebook.

A. Remembering the Facts

1. Why is it so difficult to develop a definition of E/BD that is universally accepted among professionals? (p.174-176)

2. Differentiate between infantile autism and childhood schizophrenia. (p.179,193)

3. Briefly discuss the four major factors that can be predisposing/contributing factors in the development of E/BD. (p.181-184)

4. Provide five statements that reflect current research-based knowledge regarding aggression. (p.190,191)

5. Provide several behavioral characteristics of a child who is referred to as *immature* or *withdrawn.* (p.191,192)

6. What are some of the signs of depression? When might depression lead to suicide? (p.192)

7. List and briefly describe eight characteristics of children with severe E/BD. (p.194,195)

8. Suggest four reasons why accurate *early* identification of E/BD children is almost impossible. (p.205,206)

B. Understanding the Facts

9. Why do E/BD children have such difficulty in establishing close and satisfying relationships with others? (p.172,186-193)

10. What is the significance of changing the label of *seriously emotionally disturbed* to *emotionally/behaviorally disordered*? (p.172,173)

11. What is the relationship between temperament and behavioral development? (p. 181)

12. According to recent research on controlling aggression, which types of punishment are effective? Which are not? What reasons can you suggest for this differentiation? (p.191)

13. According to the social learning theory, what is the impact of environment in the development of internalizing behaviors? (p.192)

C. Applying the Facts

14. Regarding the proposed causes of E/BD, what is the relationship between a) *cause* and *cure* b) *cause* and *blame*? (p.181-184)

15. Provide two examples of how the interactions between parents and children are *reciprocal*? (p.182)

16. What is the school's role in: a) assisting a depressed child, b) prevention of suicidal behavior? (p.192,193)

17. An underlying assumption in humanistic approaches to educating E/BD students is that these youngsters will find their own solutions to their problems if they are allowed to do so in a free and loving environment. React to this approach based on your current knowledge of the characteristics of E/BD students, as well as on your knowledge of other approaches to E/BD. (p.196-201)

18. For each of the following examples, briefly illustrate how a teacher could *intervene* using each of the five conceptual models. (p.196-201)
   a. During instruction, Bruce *drifts off* and daydreams. Consequently, he misses most of the lesson.
   b. Lisa attends for approximately half of the teacher's lesson. For the remaining half of the class, she becomes increasingly agitated and, consequently, begins to engage other children in disruptive behavior.
   c. Tom begins to cry at various times during the school day. He does not appear to be anxious to share with anyone the reasons for this behavior.
   d. The class has been instructed to line up at the door in preparation for recess. As the children proceed out of the door, Jason turns around, smashes another student's head against the wall, and rushes outdoors.

19. Suggest some ways in which to *increase* appropriate behavior in school. In addition, suggest ways in which to *decrease* inappropriate school behaviors. (p.210,211)

20. This chapter has provided many practical suggestions for general classroom teachers. Construct five statements that reflect some of the important considerations that you have learned throughout this chapter. How will these five statements guide your planning and instruction should an E/BD student be placed within your classroom?

FILL-IN-THE-BLANKS

Fill in the number of the most appropriate term listed under Terms To Note for each of the following statements.

1. Ms. Saunders, who adheres to a(n) ___ to teaching, encourages her students to find their own answers to their questions and problems. She provides a loving, supportive, and free environment.

2. Both the labels ___ and ___ are being used to describe the E/BD population.

3. Bill, aged 14, slowly shuffles into the class and sits down. The rest of the class has already started their assigned work. As he sits, he makes no attempt to get started - he doesn't even appear to be aware that the others are working. Bill is demonstrating ___.

4. Jesse 'parrots' the conversations of others. He also repeats the words *peanut butter* and *take a break* throughout the day. This characteristic is referred to as ___.

5. Ever since birth, Steven has been very easy going and pleasant. These attributes are still evident at age twelve. Because of Steven's ___ all interactions with him are pleasant.

6. Lynn, aged 16, is defiant, is rude to her parents and teachers, and is abusive to her peers. Lynn is demonstrating characteristics typical of an individual with a ___, which is a dimension of ___ .

7. In attempting to design an intervention program for an E/BD child, the teacher considers such factors as school achievement, school friendships, social skills, family structure, and relationships with parents and siblings. This teacher is using a(n) ___.

8. Genetics, socioeconomic disadvantages, and difficult family relationships can be ___ in a child being identified as E/BD. No single factor can generally be attributed to this identification. There are generally a number of ___ .

9. Ms. Cassells uses teaching techniques such as response cost, extinction, overcorrection, and rewards. She is following a(n) ___ to E/BD.

10. Barry is blind and E/BD. He is observed to be continually poking his eyes and patting his cheeks. Cindy is also E/BD. If she is left unsupervised, she will repeatedly hit her head against a wall and slap her ears. Barry is engaging in ___; whereas Cindy is engaging in ___.

11. After three months in first grade, school personnel are unaware of anyone to whom Jamie has spoken. He becomes visibly nervous whenever anyone makes any attempts to socialize with him. At recess, he wanders around the perimeter of the playground. Jamie is demonstrating characteristics typical of an individual who is displaying ___ behavior, which is a dimension of ___ .

12. Ron began to laugh when the teacher was describing an accident which involved a popular classmate. During a recent class party, Ron wandered around crying, slapping his face, and imitating animal sounds. Ron is demonstrating ___.

13. ___ is manifested prior to three years of age; whereas ___ is manifested later in life and includes hallucinations and delusions.

14. ___ has been the result of the current emphasis on both the affective and cognitive needs of E/BD students. This is seen as a viable *blend* of the conceptual models.

15. Sheila is regularly truant from school. She was recently questioned by police regarding her involvement in a robbery since she was the only suspect that the proprietor recognized. Sheila refused to provide any information on the involvement of her 'friends'. Sheila is demonstrating ___.

16. Janet has been referred to as ___ because she does not appear to have a *conscience*.

17. Mr. Piper creates a very free and permissive classroom environment. His fourth grade students are encouraged to *act out* how they feel. Mr. Piper also believes that this approach should take priority over actual teaching of academics and/or social skills. Mr. Woodward believes in a similar classroom environment, however, he places a much stronger emphasis on academic and social achievement. Mr. Piper is using a(n) ___ to education, whereas, Mr. Woodward is using a(n) ___.

18. Jeremy demonstrates a great deal of out-of-seat behavior during the day. He also 'visits' with his neighboring students when he is supposed to be completing his assigned work. Jeremy could be said to be demonstrating ___.

RETURN TO CHAPTER SUMMARY

Reread the chapter summary in the textbook (p.214,215) for an effective review of the information presented on the topic of Emotional/Behavioral Disorders.

ENRICHMENT ACTIVITIES

For your interest and further study...

1. Compare the definitions of *Behavior Disorders* at the state/provincial level and at the local school system level.

2. Observe in an educational setting for students with behavior disorders. Take specific note of the behaviors that are exhibited and the methods of intervention. Inquire of the teacher the social skill program that is being utilized.

3. Ask three general classroom teachers to share with you their 'secrets' for effective classroom management.

6

Communication Disorders

CHAPTER FOCUS

As soon as a child is born, the communication process begins. Effective communication is the essence of daily life. If, however, speech and language skills do not develop normally, this child is at risk of being unable to communicate needs and desires - in addition to experiencing stigmatization and isolation. This chapter focuses on the numerous school-age children who exhibit speech and language disorders, in addition to the teachers, parents, and other students who serve as effective *models* for these children.

CHAPTER OBJECTIVES

On completion of this chapter, the student should be able to discuss the following topics:

1. The difference between *speech disorders* and *language disorders*
2. The sequence of steps within normal speech and language development
3. The various theories of language development - with the most emphasis being placed on the pragmatic theories
4. The specific types of speech disorders
5. The various classification systems for language disorders
6. The role of the Speech-Language Pathologist
7. Strategies for assessment and intervention
8. The role of teachers and parents in overcoming and preventing speech and language difficulties
9. Alternative communication systems for severely handicapped individuals

10. The importance of early intense intervention for at-risk children
11. The unique concerns of speech/language disorders in adolescence and/or adulthood
12. General suggestions for teaching a child who demonstrates a speech or language disorder

TERMINOLOGY

Terms To Note:

The following terms are important to note. These terms will be used in a Fill-In-The-Blank exercise at the conclusion of this chapter.

1. language (p.218)
2. language disorders (p.218,220,233)
3. speech (p.218)
4. speech disorders (p.218,220,225)
5. articulation (p.221,229)
6. voice disorder (p.225,228)
7. fluency (p.221,230,231)
8. augmented communication (p.218,220,249-251)
9. phonology (p.219,220,229)
10. morphology (p.219,220)
11. syntax (p.219,220)
12. semantics (p.219,220)
13. pragmatics (p.219,220,244)
14. speech/language pathologist (p.228)
15. dysarthria (p.233)
16. apraxia (p.233)
17. acquired aphasia (p.243)

MULTIPLE CHOICE

Select the most appropriate response.

A. Remembering the Facts

1. A disability in which of the following would be indicative of a SPEECH disorder? (p.218,220)

    a. articulation and fluency
    b. language and dialect
    c. fluency and decoding
    d. social interaction

2. *Form, content,* and *function* are all important aspects of
___. (p.218,219)

    a. speech   d. phonology
    b. language   e. pragmatics
    c. pitch

3. Morphology refers to ___. (p.219,220)

    a. the construction of word forms
    b. the construction of sentences
    c. the meaning and intention of words and sentences
    d. the social use of language

4. Pragmatics refer to___. (p.219,220)

    a. the construction of word forms
    b. the construction of sentences
    c. the meaning and intention of words and sentences
    d. the social use of language

5. Semantics refer to ___. (p.219,220)

    a. the construction of word forms
    b. the construction of sentences
    c. the meaning and intention of words and sentences
    d. the social use of language

6. What percentage of exceptional American children receive
speech and language therapy? (p.221)

    a. 5%   d. 30%
    b. 10%   e. 50%
    c. 25%

7. Abnormal pitch and volume are characteristic of an
individual with a(n) ___. (p.220,225)

    a. fluency disorder   d. voice disorder
    b. articulation disorder   e. morphographical disorder
    c. language disorder

8. When a baby makes some exploratory vowel and consonant
sounds, he/she is said to be ___. (p.222,223)

    a. gooing   c. babbling
    b. echolalic   d. gurgling

9. In which list are the normal stages of communication in the correct order? (p.222,223)

    a. babbling, crying, vocal play, gooing, first words
    b. crying, babbling, gooing, vocal play, sentences
    c. crying, gooing, vocal play, babbling, first words
    d. crying, gooing, babbling, vocal play, first words

10. Most children have mastered the basic morphographical characteristics of language by age ___. (p.223)

    a. 8 months   d. 3 years
    b. 12 months   e. 5 years
    c. 18 months

11. Which of the following is NOT considered a significant factor in the development of language? (p.224)

    a. child's sex or ethnic origin
    b. physical maturation
    c. cognitive development
    d. degree of socialization

12. Pragmatic theories of language development emphasize that: (p.226,227)

    a. language is a learned response in an artificial
       setting.
    b. language develops as a natural maturational process.
    c. language is acquired through natural social
       interactions.
    d. language development is unrelated to cognitive
       development.

13. Concerning stuttering, it is known that: (p.230,231)

    a. more boys than girls will stutter.
    b. more girls than boys will stutter.
    c. stuttering is equally distributed between the sexes.
    d. 5% of all children will be stutterers.

14. Which of the following would NOT be a cause of cleft palate? (p.231)

    a. genetics
    b. trauma during fetal development
    c. brain damage
    d. abnormalities in chromosomes

15. Dysarthria and apraxia are common results of ___. (p.233)

    a. a brain injury   d. spina bifida
    b. delayed speech   e. a hearing impairment
    c. stuttering

16. Which of the following is a component of *language*? (p.233,234)

    a. listening and speaking
    b. social interaction
    c. reading and writing
    d. both a and c
    e. all of the above

17. Research by Schiefelbusch and McCormick concluded that the most useful assessment information can often be derived from: (p.243)

    a. the subjective judgment of an experienced clinician.
    b. observations of language in a variety of settings.
    c. standardized tests and developmental scales.
    d. both a and b
    e. all of the above

18. The *primary* role of the teacher in assisting children overcome speech/language problems is: (p.244)

    a. speech training.
    b. to emphasize phonology, morphology, syntax, and semantics.
    c. to enlist the assistance of parents in remediating speech and language difficulties at home.
    d. to emphasize pragmatics.

19. Headsticks, microswitches, and key guards are all associated with systems of ___. (p.249,250)

    a. augmented language
    b. articulation
    c. aphasia
    d. sign language
    e. language assessment

B. Understanding the Facts

20. Which of the following statements regarding communication disorders is TRUE? (p.218)

    a. Causes and cures of communication disorders are difficult to determine.
    b. Communication disorders often result in critical social penalties for the individual.
    c. Communication disorders are easily detected.
    d. both a and b
    e. all are true

21. With which of the following areas would an individual with a cleft palate have the LEAST amount of difficulty? (p.231,232)

    a. articulation   c. volume
    b. resonance   d. fluency

22. Children/adults with cerebral palsy would most likely demonstrate ___. (p.233)

    a. resonance difficulties
    b. articulation difficulties
    c. stuttering tendencies
    d. syntactical errors

23. Julie is four years old. As yet she has not developed useful language. Julie would NOT be considered ___. (p.238)

    a. learning disabled
    b. mentally retarded
    c. severely emotionally disturbed
    d. deaf

24. Michael is four years old. He has not as yet demonstrated any indication that he has developed receptive or expressive language. It would be most important for Michael's parents and eventual teachers to: (p.238-240)

    a. teach Michael to use pointing, or isolated words in order for him to obtain a desired result.
    b. teach Michael to phonologically reproduce all sounds and words.
    c. teach Michael sounds and words with the assistance of edible reinforcers.
    d. teach Michael to phonologically reproduce only those sounds and words that are functionally meaningful to him.
    e. both b and c
    f. both a and d

25. A child demonstrates a one year delay in language development. Which of the following would NOT be considered a cause of this delay? (p.242,243)

    a. mental retardation
    b. a learning disability
    c. a deprived environment
    d. a severe hearing loss
    e. lack of language stimulation

26. Trauma to the brain or hearing mechanism can cause a language disorder. The disabling effects of this disorder are dependent upon: (p.243)

    a. extent of injury.
    b. age of individual when injury occurred.
    c. level of language development that was intact when the injury occurred.
    d. both a and b
    e. all of the above

Applying the Facts

27. Mary says 'peas' instead of 'please'; Erin says 'sumber' instead of 'summer.' Mary and Erin are demonstrating a disorder in which subsystem of language? (p.234-236)

    a. phonology   d. semantics
    b. morphology   e. pragmatics
    c. syntax

28. Shelly tells her mother about her day at school: "We ate lunch and then we would be getting the bus off. Mr. James a nice shirt had on. Jason got sick. He looks nice with red shirts on." Shelley has difficulties with ___. (p.234-236)

    a. phonology   d. semantics
    b. morphology   e. pragmatics
    c. syntax

29. Barry has difficulty participating in the verbal bantering that is a regular occurrence during coffee breaks at work. Whenever he does attempt to participate, his 'friendly' insults are often misinterpreted as being rude and abrupt. With what subsystem of language does Barry have difficulty? (p.234-236)

    a. phonology   d. semantics
    b. morphology   e. pragmatics
    c. syntax

30. Michelle explains how to get to her friend's house: "Well, it gots a number seven and a one beside it. You go up and down in the driveroad and watch out for your cars. You go to the blue house beside the corner and turn left - no, turn right because it's right beside the other house. Her house can see a fire stinguisher from her house." In this specific situation, most of Michelle's difficulties are in the area of ___. (p.234-236)

    a. phonology   d. semantics
    b. morphology   e. pragmatics
    c. syntax

TRUE AND FALSE

Indicate whether the following statements are True or False. In your notebook, rewrite the False statements so that they are accurate.

1. Communication disorders, in comparison to other exceptionalities, are relatively simple in cause and cure. (p.218)   T   F

2. Communication always involves language. (p.218)   T   F

3. Most children with language disorders have speech difficulties, however, it is possible to have appropriate phonology and poor language. (p.218,219)   T   F

4. According to the pragmatic theories of language development, the social environment should provide the cues, motivation, rewards, and practice required for language development. (p.224,226,227)   T   F

5. Due to the recent mainstreaming emphasis, speech/language pathologists will be providing more assistance to communication disordered children in more restrictive settings. (p.228)   T   F

6. Stuttering is the most frequent type of fluency disorder. (p.230,231)   T   F

7. Causes of stuttering are fairly easy to determine. In addition, appropriate treatment for stuttering is fairly simple to implement. (p.230,231)   T   F

8. The most common orofacial defect in children is cleft lip/palate. (p.231)   T   F

9. Parents can assist their nonverbal child in acquiring functional language by providing numerous opportunities to use language. (p.238-240)   T   F

10. Standardized testing appears to be one of the most useful tools in language assessment. (p.243,244)   T   F

11. A child who is struggling to learn English as a second language would be considered to be language disordered. (p.220,251,252)   T   F

12. The most effective speech/language interventions are implemented in the *natural* environments of young children. (p.253)   T   F

SHORT ANSWER QUESTIONS

Answer the following questions in your notebook.

A. Remembering the Facts

1. State three reasons why the prevalence of communication disorders is difficult to establish. (p.221,234)

2. Briefly summarize the normal development of language in a child from birth to eight years of age. (p.221-223)

3. Differentiate between disorders of phonation and disorders of resonance. (p.225)

4. Differentiate between speech disorders and language disorders. What is the reason for the increased focus on language disorders? (p.218,220,233)

5. Briefly describe the four types of language disorders as suggested by Naremore. (p.238-243)

6. Explain early attempts to teach language to nonverbal children. What methods are currently employed? What does the research suggest concerning both of these methods? (p.238-242)

7. What is sociodramatic play? (p.253)

B. Understanding the Facts

8. All children make articulation and/or phonological errors. When do these errors constitute a *disorder*? (p.229)

9. Research by the authors has lead to some conclusions regarding the language of learning disabled children. Provide five summarizing statements that reflect these recent conclusions. (p.241,242)

10. Describe how sociodramatic play could be effectively utilized at various grade levels? (p.253)

C. Applying the Facts

11. Your friend is the parent of a 20 month old child who has already demonstrated cognitive and sensory deficits. Provide a list of helpful suggestions to assist this parent in facilitating this child's maximum language potential. (p.252,253)

12. This chapter has provided many practical suggestions for general classroom teachers. Construct five statements that reflect some of the important considerations that you have learned throughout this chapter. How will these five statements guide your planning should a student with a communication disorder be placed within your classroom?

FILL-IN-THE-BLANKS

Fill in the number of the most appropriate term listed under <u>Terms To Note</u> for each of the following statements.

1. Statements such as, "Last week we swimmeded"; or "There are 27 childrens in our class" are indicative of a problem with ___.

2. Impairments in the production and use of *oral* language are known as ___.

3. Consider the following sentences: With who do you want to go with? Mother packed things for swimming, for fishing, and a lunch to eat. Both of these sentences reflect errors in ___.

4. Keith, who has cerebral palsy, is of average intelligence and academic achievement. Because he is quadriplegic, he requires a(n) ___ system to assist with communication.

5. Jessica experiences difficulty with reading body language. She also experiences embarrassment when she does not recognize the punch line of jokes. Jessica has a problem with ___.

6. Carl has a very loud and irritating voice. Jason speaks with a monotone. Cathy speaks with a *sing-song* type of inflection. All of these children are demonstrating a(n) ___.

7. Jill, age 5, was a victim of a serious auto accident in which she sustained a major head injury. After a period of recovery, it was observed that Jill's language skills were severely impaired. Jill was diagnosed as having ___.

8. ___ is the communication of *ideas* through an arbitrary system of symbols and rules, whereas ___ is the physical behavior of producing sounds.

9. Joe (aged 13) and his father have just returned from a fantastic fishing trip. When asked how the trip was, Joe replied, "Oh, man, it was *nasty*!" On hearing this, his father's face fell, and he retorted, "What do you mean - *nasty*? It was *great*!" It wasn't until Joe's mother intervened and asked each of them to define their terms that they realized that they were talking about the same thing! Joe and his father were having difficulty with ___.

10. Neurological damage can cause ___, which interferes with the articulation of speech sounds, or ___ which makes the selection and sequencing of speech difficult.

11. Jenny continually adds the syllable *uh* at the conclusion of many of her words, e.g., "M*yuh* frien*duh* is*uh* coming t*ouh* m*yuh* house." Karen has just lost her two front teeth and has difficulty with the *'s'* sound. Jenny has a(n) ___ problem, whereas, Karen has a temporary ___ problem.

12. Leslie is not a teacher, but performs most of her professional responsibilities within a classroom. She provides assistance to many children including preschool children, learning disabled children, and children with multiple disabilities. She is a member of ASHA. Leslie is a(n) ___.

13. Robert calls himself, "Wobert." He has a difficulty with ___.

14. The social penalties of ___ are much more debilitating than speech disorders.

RETURN TO CHAPTER SUMMARY

Reread the chapter summary in the textbook (p.260,261) for a review of the information presented in Chapter Six.

ENRICHMENT ACTIVITIES

1. Observe a speech/language assessment. If possible, observe the follow-up discussion with the parents and teacher with regard to remedial activities.

2. Act as a speech/language aid under the direction of a speech/language pathologist.

3. Develop an auditory tape that demonstrates examples of the various speech/language problems that are experienced by young children.

7

Hearing Impairment

CHAPTER FOCUS

Children with hearing impairments present special challenges
to educators because of the accompanying interference with
language development and communication skills. Chapter
seven provides suggestions for educators when interacting
with deaf and hard of hearing students.

CHAPTER OBJECTIVES

On completion of this chapter, the student should be able to
discuss the following topics:

1. The difference among the terms *deafness*, *hard of hearing*
    and *hearing impairment*
2. The criteria for the educational and physiological
    classifications of hearing impairment
3. The prevalence of hearing impairments
4. The basic anatomy of the ear, specifically the
    significance of each part of the ear in the process of
    hearing
5. Three general types of hearing tests
6. Major causes of hearing loss
7. How a hearing impairment impacts upon speech and
    language development, cognitive development, academic
    achievement, and social development
8. Oral, manual, and total communication systems that are
    commonly used
9. Placement options for hearing impaired students
10. Recent technological advances that provide assistance
    to hearing impaired individuals
11. A rationale for effective academic programs at the
    preschool and postsecondary levels

12. General suggestions and procedures for teaching a
    hearing impaired student in a general education
    classroom and/or within a community school

TERMINOLOGY

Terms To Note:

The following terms are important to note. These terms will
be used in a Fill-In-The-Blank exercise at the conclusion of
this chapter.

    1. decibels (p.266)
    2. deaf (p.266)
    3. hard of hearing (p.266)
    4. hearing impairment (p.266)
    5. congenitally deaf (p.266)
    6. adventitiously deaf (p.266)
    7. prelingual deafness (p.266)
    8. postlingual deafness (p.266)
    9. tympanic membrane (p.267)
   10. auricle (p.267)
   11. ossicles (p.268)
   12. malleus (p.268)
   13. stapes (p.268)
   14. incus (p.268)
   15. oval window (p.268)
   16. vestibular mechanism (p.268)
   17. cochlea (p.268)
   18. pure-tone audiometry (p.268,269)
   19. Hertz units (p.268,269)
   20. speech audiometry (p.269,270)
   21. speech reception threshold (p.269,270)
   22. play audiometry (p.270)
   23. reflex audiometry (p.270)
   24. evoked-response audiometry (p.270)
   25. conductive hearing loss (p.271)
   26. sensorineural hearing loss (p.271)
   27. mixed hearing loss (p.271)
   28. audiogram (p.271)
   29. speech intelligibility (p.274)
   30. deaf culture (p.277,278)
   31. total communication approach (p.278)
   32. auditory training (p.279)
   33. speechreading (p.279)
   34. homophenes (p.283)
   35. fingerspelling (p.283,284)
   36. signing English systems (p.283,284)
   37. American Sign Language (p.284,285)
   38. television captioning (p.288)
   39. teletypewriter (p.288,289)
   40. group auditory trainers (p.289)

MULTIPLE CHOICE

Select the most appropriate response.

A. Remembering the Facts

1. In reading an audiological report, an educator would be most interested in: (p.266)

    a. how the hearing loss affects the student's ability to communicate and develop language.
    b. the age of onset of the hearing loss.
    c. the decibel level of hearing loss.
    d. both a and b
    e. both a and c

2. Prevalence estimates for hearing impaired children show variance because of: (p.267)

    a. differences in definitions and classification systems.
    b. accuracy of testing instruments.
    c. differences within the population studied.
    d. both a and c
    e. all of the above

3. Which part of the ear is MOST important for hearing? (p.268)

    a. tympanic membrane   c. stapes
    b. cochlea   d. vestibular mechanism

4. Speech audiometry measures: (p.269,270)

    a. an individual's ability to detect and understand speech.
    b. an individual's threshold for hearing a variety of speech sounds.
    c. an individual's ability to imitate speech sounds.
    d. an individual's sensitivity to pure tones.

5. Speech detection is: (p.269)

    a. the highest level that speech can be detected without understanding.
    b. the lowest level that speech can be detected with understanding.
    c. the lowest level that speech can be detected without understanding.
    d. the highest level that speech can be detected with understanding.

6. Which of the following is NOT an impairment of the outer ear? (p.271)

   a. otitis media   c. buildup of cerumen
   b. swimmer's ear   d. atresia

7. The most common middle ear problem is ___. (p.271,272)

   a. external otitis   d. otitis media
   b. tumors   e. cytomegalovirus
   c. roaring or ringing noises

8. The most severe hearing loss occurs as a result of damage or problems with ___. (p.271,272)

   a. the outer ear   c. the inner ear
   b. the middle ear

9. Which of the following results in the LEAST devastating hearing impairment? (p.271-274)

   a. hereditary factors   c. meningitis
   b. otitis media   d. maternal rubella

10. On what does a hearing impairment have the GREATEST impact? (p.274)

   a. social adjustment   c. reading ability
   b. language development   d. cognitive development

11. The major reason for poor speech and language development in hearing impaired children is ___. (p.274)

   a. lack of feedback
   b. lack of parental and teacher support
   c. lack of 'babbling ability'
   d. lack of the mechanisms of speech production
   e. lack of stimuli

12. Which academic area is most significantly affected by a hearing impairment? (p.276)

   a. mathematics   d. social studies
   b. spelling   e. writing
   c. reading

13. The major difference between speechreading and lipreading is: (p.279)

   a. a different language is used in speechreading.
   b. a different sign language is used in lipreading.
   c. a different intensity and frequency of sound is used in speechreading.
   d. a different environment is used in speechreading.

14. Auditory training attempts to assist hearing impaired individuals with all of the following EXCEPT: (p.279,280)

    a. speechreading.
    b. awareness of sounds.
    c. discrimination among speech sounds.
    d. discrimination among environmental sounds.

15. Since the implementation of PL94-142, approximately ___ of hearing impaired students are enrolled in general education classrooms. (p.285,286)

    a. 10%   d. 40%
    b. 20%   e. 50%
    c. 30%

B. Understanding the Facts

16. The basic difference between the physiological and educational viewpoints concerning the categories of hearing impairment is: (p.265,266)

    a. the method of audiological assessment.
    b. the method in which the results of the audiological
       assessment are interpreted.
    c. the implications for home intervention.
    d. both a and b
    e. there is no difference between these viewpoints

17. Prevalence estimates are difficult to establish, however, it appears that approximately ___ school children is/are identified as having a hearing impairment. (p.362)

    a. 1 out of every 10,000
    b. 10 out of every 1000
    c. 1 out of every 1000
    d. 10 out of every 10,000

18. Linda is able to participate in conversations if they are loud enough, however, she is 'lost' within a class discussion. She has a limited vocabulary and her speech is somewhat defective in spite of intense training. According to Table 7-1 on page 275, Linda has a ___ hearing impairment.

    a. slight   d. severe
    b. mild   e. extreme
    c. marked

19. Learning to speechread can be difficult for some students because: (p.279)

    a. many hearing impaired students have low cognitive
       ability.
    b. it requires the use of a separate system of grammar.
    c. it is not socially acceptable.
    d. there are many homophenes in speech.

C. Applying the Facts

20. Jonathan has profound mental retardation and displays autistic tendencies. Because of his inattentiveness and unresponsiveness, his parents would like to know if he also has a hearing impairment. Which of the following tests would provide the most USEFUL information? (p.268-270)

    a. pure-tone audiometry   d. play audiometry
    b. speech audiometry   e. reflex audiometry
    c. evoked-response audiometry

21. Carolyn has a mild hearing loss. With just this piece of information, which of the following would probably most accurately describe Carolyn? (p.275)

    a. She will definitely need to wear hearing aids.
    b. She will have defective speech and will need to learn
       a system of signing.
    c. She will have difficulty with distant and/or faint
       speech.
    d. She will be unable to hear conversations unless
       they are very loud.

22. Stewart, age 10 months, is totally deaf. How much speech will he develop WITHOUT extensive training? (p.274)

    a. some intelligible speech
    b. no intelligible speech
    c. some barely intelligible speech

23. Margaret uses speechreading in the regular classroom. To facilitate speechreading, Margaret's teacher should: (p.282)

    a. wear an FM system.
    b. keep within a close distance of her.
    c. always exaggerate facial gestures and body language.
    d. never use the blackboard.

24. Michael, age 5, has a 58 dB hearing loss. He has no other exceptionalities. The *best* educational placement for Michael would be a: (p.275,287)

    a. full-time regular classroom.
    b. full-time self-contained classroom.
    c. regular classroom with resource assistance three times per week.
    d. self-contained classroom with integration into a regular classroom on a daily basis.
    e. self-contained classroom with social integration into a regular classroom several times a week.

MATCHING

Match each of the following aural conditions with the correct description: (p.271-273)

a. atresia
b. external otitis
c. otitis media

d. nonsupportive otitis media
e. otosclerosis
f. cytomegalovirus

1. ___ is an infection of the middle ear and can result in a ruptured eardrum.
2. ___ is a virus among newborns and is difficult to diagnose.
3. ___ is often preceded by otitis media.
4. ___ occurs when the external auditory canal does not form.
5. ___ is another name for 'swimmer's ear'.
6. ___ occurs when the stapes become attached to the oval window.

TRUE AND FALSE

Indicate whether the following statements are True or False. In your notebook, rewrite the False statements so that they are accurate.

1. From an educational viewpoint concerning hearing impairments, there is greater concern over the development of language and communication skills than concern over the decibel measure of hearing loss. (p.265,266)   T   F

2. A hearing threshold of 72 dB would be considered to be in the 'severe' classification of hearing impairment. (p.266,275)   T   F

3. A person with normal hearing can clearly determine a sound at 0 dB. (p.266)   T   F

4. Middle ear problems rarely result in deafness and are often correctable. (p.271,272)   T   F

5. Childhood deafness is most commonly the result of hereditary factors. (p.272)   T   F

6. A child with a slight or mild hearing loss is more likely to be *overlooked* than a child who has a more severe loss. (p.275) T   F

7. There is a higher prevalence of emotional disturbance and social maladjustment in the hearing impaired population than in the hearing population. (p.276,277)   T   F

8. At the present time, most educators prefer to use the total communication approach as opposed to exclusive use of either the oral or manual methods. (p.278)   T   F

9. Speechreading is a more accurate term than lipreading. (p.279)   T   F

10. Auditory training will assist the hearing impaired child to 'hear better'. (p.279,282)   T   F

11. Signing English systems are the same as American Sign Language. (p.283,284)   T   F

12. All hearing impaired children are assisted by the use of hearing aids. (p.289)   T   F

SHORT ANSWER QUESTIONS

Answer the following questions in your notebook.

A. Remembering the Facts

1. Distinguish among the four terms: congenitally deaf; adventitiously deaf; prelingual deafness; postlingual deafness. (p.266)

2. Describe three methods of assessing the hearing ability of very young and hard to test children. (p.270)

3. Explain the difference between a conductive hearing loss and a sensorineural hearing loss. (p.271)

4. What are the advantages and disadvantages of telephone adaptions for hearing impaired individuals? (p.288,289)

5. List the 'warning flags' that should alert a teacher/parent to the possibility of a hearing impairment in a child.   (p.294)

6. List five ways of improving oral instruction with hearing impaired students.   (p.295)

B. Understanding the Facts

7. What is the difference between speech detection and speech reception?   Why is this difference important for teachers?   (p.269,270)

8. According to the authors, it is a greater disadvantage to be hearing impaired than visually impaired.   Why? Do you agree?   (p.274)

9. Make a general statement regarding the intellectual ability of hearing impaired individuals.   What factors may impact on intellectual development and performance on an intelligence test?   (p.275,276)

10. What would be the advantages and disadvantages of both an integrated school setting and a segregated school setting for a hearing impaired student?   (p.285-287)

11. Why is early intervention a positive step for hearing impaired children?   What would be the nature of effective early intervention for: a) a mild loss,   b) a severe loss?   (p.275,287,290,292)

12. Identify some of the problems faced by hearing impaired adults in the workplace.   (p.293)

C. Applying the Facts

13. Why is there a difference of opinion concerning the dividing point between prelingual and postlingual deafness?   (p.266)

14. Given a hearing impaired student's difficulty with speech, language, and reading ability, what does the research suggest as a method of improving achievement?   (p.276)   What teaching techniques 'fit' with this teaching methodology?   (p.294-296)

15. Suggest ways in which social interaction and acceptance can be enhanced for hearing impaired students in the school system.   How can mainstreaming be utilized in this process?   (p.276,277,286)

16. This chapter has provided many practical suggestions for general classroom teachers. Write five statements that reflect what you have learned about hearing impaired individuals. How will this information guide your planning and teaching should a hearing impaired student be placed within your classroom?

FILL-IN-THE-BLANKS

Fill in the number of the most appropriate term listed under Terms To Note for each of the following statements.

1. In order to test Jason's hearing level, it was necessary to sedate him and measure brain-wave activity. This is referred to as ___ .

2. The most visible part of the ear is known as the ___ .

3. The combination of oral and manual methods of communication is known as the ___ .

4. Another name for ___ is 'FM systems.'

5. Loudness (intensity, of sounds) is measured in ___ , whereas frequency (number of vibrations) of sounds is measured in ___ . Both of these measures are provided by ___ .

6. ___ is a true language that has its own grammar.

7. More important than their religion, their mother tongue, and their country of birth is the focus on their *deafness*. Because of this narrow focus on their exceptionality, a(n) ___ has emerged.

8. Kathy was diagnosed as 'deaf' when she was four months old. Steven suffered an extreme case of otitis media at age five, leaving him with a profound hearing loss (over 90 dB). Kathy would be described as having ___ , whereas Steven's condition has left him with ___ .

9. A student who is ___ will have much more difficulty in the development of language than a student who is ___ .

10. Ken has a hearing loss of 50 dB in one ear and a 80 dB loss in the other ear. With the assistance of hearing aids, Ken can understand linguistic information. Ken is ___ .

11. If a deaf person did not know the correct sign for your name, he/she would probably use ___ to introduce you to another deaf person.

12. The terms ___ and lipreading cannot be used interchangeably because lipreading utilizes only the movement of the mouth.

13. In ___, the examiner attempts to motivate the examinee by utilizing a 'game' format.

14. Mary cannot be assisted by hearing aids. Her audiological report states that she has a hearing loss of 105 dB. Mary would be considered ___.

15. Audiologists, in order to determine the severity of a hearing loss, need to determine the location of the hearing problem. A(n) ___ is very useful for this purpose.

16. Sound waves are transferred from the middle ear to the inner ear via the ___.

17. ___ has allowed a hearing impaired individual to enjoy a wide range of television programs. The ___ has provided this individual with telephone access.

18. The part of the ear that is essential for maintaining a sense of balance is the ___.

19. ___ will assist a hearing impaired child in being as efficient as possible in utilizing the hearing that he/she possesses.

20. A(n) ___ is the result of problems of the outer and/or middle ear. Alternatively, impairment of the inner ear would result in a(n) ___. When the outer, middle, and inner ear are affected, a(n) ___ results.

21. The ___, which is the most important organ for hearing, converts vibrations into electrical signals that are transmitted to the brain.

22. Due to age and/or additional exceptionalities, some children can be assessed for hearing loss by monitoring their responses to loud sudden noises. Another name for this method is ___.

23. The words 'me' and 'be' would be easily confused by a speechreader because they 'look' the same. Words such as these are called ___.

24. Mary (in #14) and Ken (in #10) both have a(n) ___.

25. Another name for the eardrum is the ___.

26. Through the use of ___, it was determined that Sarah can detect speech at 80 dB but cannot understand speech at that level. Providing an estimate of ___ would give Sarah's parents and teachers more useful information.

27. The tympanic membrane and three ___ (known as the ___, ___, and ___) make up the middle ear.

28. The milder the hearing loss, the greater the ___.

29. ___ are a form of manual communication that is used in the total communication approach and have been designed for the purpose of teaching deaf individuals to communicate.

RETURN TO CHAPTER SUMMARY

Reread the chapter summary in the textbook (p.298,299) in order to review the information presented regarding Hearing Impairments.

ENRICHMENT ACTIVITIES

For your interest and further study...

1. Consult with the supervisor of student services at a local college or university. Determine the services that are available for hard of hearing and/or deaf students.

2. As a matter of interest, have your own hearing ability assessed both through the screening procedures available within a local school system and by an audiologist who utilizes a soundproof booth.

8

Visual Impairment

CHAPTER FOCUS

This chapter focuses on a visually impaired student's ability, not disability. Attention is given to curriculum adaptations and modifications that are necessary for effective programming.

CHAPTER OBJECTIVES

On completion of this chapter, the student should be able to discuss the following topics:

1. The definitional differences among the terms *legal blindness, educational blindness, partially sighted*, and *low vision*
2. Current vision testing procedures
3. The visual process
4. Refractive errors
5. Diseases that can effect the visual system
6. Language development in visually impaired children
7. The intellectual ability and academic achievement of visually impaired students
8. Concept development of visually impaired students
9. The importance of mobility skills
10. Important considerations in social adjustment for visually impaired students
11. Curriculum adaptations and modifications that are necessary for visually impaired students
12. Technological advances for the visually impaired individual
13. Educational placements for visually impaired students
14. The importance of the preschool years

15. The development of employment skills that are essential for visually impaired adolescents and adults
16. Suggestions and procedures for the effective teaching of visually impaired students in general education classrooms

TERMINOLOGY

Terms to Note:

The following terms are important to note. These terms will be used in a Fill-In-The-Blank exercise at the conclusion of this chapter.

1. legal definition of blindness (p.302,304)
2. educational definition of blindness (p.304)
3. partially sighted (p.304)
4. low vision (p.304)
5. cornea (p.305)
6. aqueous humor (p.305)
7. pupil (p.305)
8. iris (p.305)
9. lens (p.305)
10. vitreous humor (p.305)
11. retina (p.305)
12. Snellen chart (p.305,306)
13. visual efficiency (p.306)
14. Diagnostic Assessment Procedure (p.306)
15. myopia (p.306)
16. hyperopia (p.306)
17. astigmatism (p.306)
18. synthetic touch (p.309)
19. analytic touch (p.309)
20. cognitive mapping (p.310,311)
21. stereotypic behaviors (p.313)
22. Braille (p.318)
23. Perkins Brailler (p.318)
24. slate and stylus (p.318)
25. Laser cane (p.325)
26. Sonicguide (p.326)
27. Optacon (p.328)
28. Kurzweil Reading Machine (p.328)
29. Versabraille (p.328)
30. Cranmer abacus (p.330)

MULTIPLE CHOICE

Select the most appropriate response.

A. Remembering the Facts

1. Which of the following has NOT been determined as a reliable method of assessing a blind individual's IQ? (p.308,309)

   a. the Verbal scale of the Wechsler tests
   b. the Performance Scale on the Wechsler tests
   c. Hayes Stanford-Binet
   d. Blind Learning Aptitude Test (BLAT)
   e. none of the above

2. Which statement is TRUE? (p.310,311)

   a. Motivation to get around is one of the major factors involved in mobility efficiency for a visually impaired person.
   b. Mobility is usually more efficient for those individuals who have a fair amount of residual vision.
   c. Mobility efficiency is much more pronounced in those individuals who become blind later in life.
   d. all are true
   e. none are true

3. Training partially sighted students to use their remaining vision: (p.319,320)

   a. will result in students being able to see better.
   b. will result in students harming their eyes.
   c. will result in students becoming more efficient in using the vision they have.
   d. is not as effective as having the students learn to read Braille.

4. One of the major disadvantages of the recent technology explosion in instructional aids for the visually impaired is: (p.328)

   a. the impracticality of the aids.
   b. the expense of the aids.
   c. the extensive training necessary for using the aids.
   d. the poor accessibility of the aids.

5. The Optacon produces ___. (p.328)

   a. compressed speech
   b. Braille dots
   c. enlarged print images on a screen
   d. ultrasonic sounds
   e. vibrating images of letters

6. The majority of visually impaired students spend most of their school day in ___ (p.330)

   a. a resource room
   b. a regular classroom
   c. a residential school
   d. a special classroom

7. What type of intervention appears to be critical in the academic future of a visually impaired child? (p.331,332)

   a. parental training and support
   b. early intervention
   c. intense intervention
   d. a and b
   e. all of the above

B. Understanding the Facts

8. Which statement is TRUE? (p.302,304)

   a. A legally blind person is also considered educationally blind.
   b. An educationally blind person is also considered legally blind.
   c. The terms *legally blind* and *educationally blind* are interchangeable.

9. Which of the following would be a good reason for not solely basing educational decisions solely on the results of the Snellen chart? (p.305,306)

   a. The Snellen chart does not predict how a child will use print materials.
   b. The Snellen chart does not measure field of vision.
   c. The Snellen chart does not assess visual functioning.
   d. a and b
   e. all are good reasons

10. Caution must be exercised when assessing the IQ of blind individuals using instruments that are normally used with sighted individuals because: (p.308,309)

    a. the modifications made on the test will affect the validity of the results.
    b. only certain parts of the test can be appropriately used with the blind.
    c. the standardization may not contain any blind individuals.
    d. b and c
    e. all of the above

11. Social skills training is an essential component in an educational program for a visually impaired student because: (p.313)

    a. a visually impaired student will not learn social skills as 'automatically' as will a sighted student.
    b. a visually impaired student is more 'at risk' of being unaccepted by society if their social skills are not intact.
    c. a visually impaired student is generally maladjusted due to his/her impairment.
    d. a and b only
    e. all of the above

12. Which one of the following four general methods of mobility would provide the greatest safety for the visually impaired traveller? (p.322-327)

    a. human guide   c. long cane
    b. guide dog   d. electronic guide

13. Which one of the following four general methods of mobility would require the most maintenance, care, and training? (p.322-327)

    a. human guide   c. long cane
    b. guide dog   d. electronic guide

C. Applying the Facts

14. Which student would be classified as *educationally blind*? (p.302,304)

    a. Tom uses a magnifier in order to read his textbooks.
    b. Susan tapes her history lecture and at the same time takes point-form notes with a slate and stylus.
    c. Randy uses a large print math text and records all answers with a black felt-tip pen.
    d. Meagan sits at the front of the classroom in order to read the chalkboard notes.

15. In a school system of 10,000 students, which of the following prevalence estimates would most accurately describe the number of students identified as visually impaired? (p.304)

   a. 1 - 3   c. 7 - 10
   b. 4 - 6   d. 11 - 20

16. Joe's measure of acuity on the Snellen Chart is 20/200 in both eyes. His vision can be corrected with lenses to 20/20 in both eyes. Which of the following conditions best describes Joe? (p.302,304)

   a. sighted   c. partially sighted
   b. legally blind   d. educationally blind

17. Mr. Wright teaches 11 visually impaired students. These students live in their own homes and spend their entire school day with Mr. Wright in one classroom specifically designed for visually impaired students. Mr. Wright is a(n) ___. (p.330)

   a. special class teacher   c. resource teacher
   b. itinerant teacher   d. residential school teacher

18. Ms. Sawyer is responsible for 15 visually impaired students. All of these students live in their own homes and attend school in their own communities. The majority of their day is spent in a regular classroom. Ms. Sawyer visits each student on a regular basis, working with each student and/or consulting with the general classroom teacher. Ms. Sawyer is a(n) ___. (p.330)

   a. resource teacher   c. special class teacher
   b. itinerant teacher   d. residential school teacher

19. Which of the following administrative arrangements for visually impaired students would be the most RESTRICTIVE? (p.330)

   a. residential school   d. special classroom
   b. resource room   e. regular classroom
   c. itinerant teacher program

20. Linda is visually impaired. She is enrolled in a regular classroom. The best way for her teacher and classmates to treat Linda is: (p.337,338)

    a. to seldom allow her to experience failure.
    b. to give her special attention whenever possible.
    c. to avoid having her compete with the other students in the class.
    d. to not pamper her or treat her differently than the other students.
    e. to give her a special curriculum.

MATCHING

Match each of the following eye conditions with the correct description. (p.306-308)

a. Glaucoma
b. Cataract
c. Diabetic Retinopathy
d. Coloboma

e. Nystagmus
f. Retinitis Pigmentosa
g. Retinopathy of Prematurity *BABIES*
h. Strabismus

1. _G_ is considered to be an *environmental* condition that leads to blindness.
2. _C_ is the direct result of another disease.
3. _A_ results in extreme pressure in the eyeball.
4. _H_ is another name for 'crossed eyes'.
5. _B_ blur vision by clouding the lens of the eye.
6. _F_ results in 'tunnel vision'.
7. _E_ is characterized by continuous involuntary eye movement.
8. _D_ results from an incomplete formation of the retina.

TRUE AND FALSE

Indicate whether the following statements are True or False. In your notebook, rewrite the False statements so that they are accurate.

1. The majority of *blind* people have some degree of useful vision. (p.302-304)   (T)   F

2. For an individual to be labelled *legally blind*, both acuity and field of vision must be impaired. (p.302,304) T   (F)

3. There are more blind adults than blind children. (p.304)
(T)   F

4. Mary's visual acuity is 20/200. Susan's visual acuity is 20/70. Susan has better visual acuity. (p.305,306)   (T)   F

5. Field of vision is most often measured with the Snellen chart. (p.305,306)   T   (F)

6. More comprehensive information about a student's visual ability would be provided by the Diagnostic Assessment Procedure than the Snellen chart.   (p.305,306)   (T)   F

7. The language development of visually impaired children differs significantly from that of their sighted peers. (p.308)   T   (F)

8. The Blind Learning Aptitude Test is primarily a verbal test. (p.308)   T   (F)

9. Blind individuals have the advantage of using obstacle sense as well as a greater acuity in the other senses. (p.311,312)   T   (F)

10. Research substantiates that, in general, blind individuals have superior musical ability compared to sighted individuals. (p.312)   T   (F)

11. A partially sighted student is at risk for harming his/her eyes to an even greater extent by using the eyes too much. (p.319,320)   T   (F)

12. Blind infants lack the motivation to explore their environment and therefore can be somewhat delayed in motor development. (p.331,332)   (T)   F

13. Simulated work settings in a classroom are not as conducive to 'success on the job' as regular work settings. (p. 334,335)   (T)   F

SHORT ANSWER QUESTIONS

Answer the following questions in your notebook.

A. Remembering the Facts

1. The authors suggest three reasons why visual impairments tend to evoke some degree of awkwardness in the sighted population. Briefly discuss these three reasons. (p.302)

2. List some of the symptoms of potential eye problems for which a teacher/parent should be watching. (p.307)

3. Briefly describe the three competing theories of the causes of stereotypic behavior in visually impaired individuals. Provide a summarizing statement that would best describe why stereotypic behavior occurs. (p.313,315)

4. Briefly summarize five reasons why Braille may not be the most efficient method of gaining information. (p.318)

5. Explain the significance of early intense education for visually impaired children. (p.331,332)

B. Understanding the Facts

6. How could the legal definition of visual impairment be misleading to educators? How can the educational definition, although not as precise, be more of a guide to educators? (p.302,304)

7. Why would the use of a blindfold on a sighted person not be an absolutely true representation of blindness as it is experienced by most 'blind' individuals? (p.303-305)

8. For what academic tasks would Braille reading and writing be more efficient than tape recordings? When would tape recordings be more efficient than Braille? (p.318-322)

C. Applying the Facts

9. The mother of a blind child makes the following statement: "My child has better hearing than a sighted child." In what way is this mother correct? In what way is this mother incorrect? Reword this mother's statement to reflect what you know about sensory acuteness in visually impaired individuals. (p.311,312,322)

10. What reason might there be behind the fact that many Braille users are very poor spellers? (p.318,319)

11. List some of the advantages and disadvantages of a residential placement (as opposed to a more integrated setting) for: (p.330)
    a) an average or above average visually impaired student
    b) a multihandicapped visually impaired student

12. This chapter has provided many practical suggestions for general classroom teachers. Construct five statements that would reflect some of the important considerations you have learned throughout this chapter. How will these five statements guide your planning should a visually impaired student be placed within your classroom?

FILL-IN-THE-BLANKS

Fill in the number of the most appropriate term listed under <u>Terms To Note</u> for each of the following statements.

1. Marg has no difficulty reading her school textbooks and using the computer. She cannot, however, read the chalkboard unless she is very close to the front of the classroom. Marg has ___.

2. Darryl is partially sighted. Because of his ___, he is able to locate his red jacket in the closet and can also pick the raisins out of a bran muffin.

3. Head banging, body rocking, and eye rubbing are examples of ___ that are exhibited by visually impaired individuals as well as by severely retarded or disturbed individuals.

4. The ___ of the eye can refract in order for an image to be focused on the retina.

5. To be labeled 'blind', the ___ requires that a student use a tactual or auditory method of reading and writing. The ___ is more precise and sets specific quantities on acuity and field of vision before the label 'blind' can be used.

6. The ___ is a very common measure of central visual acuity.

7. Beth has difficulty in viewing the movie screen, reading her textbooks, and setting the combination of her lock. Her optometrist has prescribed a corrective lens. Beth has ___.

8. Teaching a blind child what a city bus 'looks like' would require ___, whereas, teaching this child what a telephone 'looks like' would require ___.

9. The colored muscular partition of the eye that expands and contracts to regulate the amount of light admitted into the eye is the ___.

10. A student who has been labeled *educationally blind* would make use of a(n) ___ in order to take notes in class. This tool is not as cumbersome or as audible as the Braillewriter.

11. John does not experience any difficulty in playing volleyball. However, when playing his favorite computer games with his friends, John wears the glasses that were prescribed to him. John has ___.

12. Located at the back of the eyeball is the ___ which translates the ray of light into an image that we call 'seeing'.

13. Mary uses ___ along with her cassette player and computer in order to read and write Braille more efficiently.

14. Even though the slate and stylus are much easier to transport and less audible, the ___ is much easier to learn to use when learning to write Braille.

15. The ___ can transpose print materials into tactile letters, whereas the ___ can convert print into synthesized speech.

16. Light rays are focused onto the retina by the ___.

17. Most individuals who are labeled *legally blind* are ___ because they have some degree of useful vision.

18. In an effort to provide a more comprehensive assessment tool for visual efficiency, Barraga developed the ___.

19. The watery substance within the eye is called ___, whereas the gelatinous substance is referred to as ___.

20. Terry, who is educationally blind, has noted that the teacher's desk is to the right of the classroom door. He has also noted that his own desk is at the end of the row of desks that are to the right of the teacher's desk. Terry is using a method of ___ to aid in mobility.

21. The ___ is the central opening in the eye.

22. The ___ and the ___ are two mobility aids that utilize the conversion of light reflections into sound waves.

23. Learning to read ___ is much more difficult than learning to read print.

24. Visually impaired individuals who can read print with the aid of a magnifier or large print are referred to as having ___.

25. Talking calculators and the ___ are two mathematical aids for visually impaired individuals.

RETURN TO CHAPTER SUMMARY

Reread the chapter summary in the textbook (p.340,341) for a helpful review of information presented on the topic of Visual Impairments.

ENRICHMENT ACTIVITIES

For your interest and further study...

1. Consult with a local ophthalmologist/optometrist in order to learn:
        a. the elements of an eye examination
        b. assessment procedures for low vision students

2. Contact your local resource center for educational materials and examine some large print and Braille textbooks. Also, listen to some recordings that utilize compressed speech.

3. Wearing a blindfold, attempt some of the following activities:
   a) make a sandwich   d) eat a meal
   b) make your bed   e) wash dishes
   c) select and put on your clothing

   Even though being blindfolded isn't what being blind is really like, comment on how you felt, how the activity went, and what adaptations would have to be made to facilitate the activity in future attempts.

4. Check out your community for special services to visually impaired individuals. Offer your services as a volunteer to record talking books, to be a reader for a visually impaired student, to act as a sighted guide, or to assist in preparing Braille materials for students in your community.

5. How has your community prepared for visually handicapped individuals? Identify some potential accessibility problems for visually impaired individuals. Some places to check are elevators, transit systems, libraries.

6. Spend some time thinking about various sporting activities that most individuals enjoy - either in active or passive participation. What about visually impaired children and adults? Can sporting activities be adapted or modified for this population? In what aspects of a sporting activity could a visually impaired individual participate?

9

Physical Disabilities

CHAPTER FOCUS

This chapter addresses the needs of children whose physical limitations and/or health problems interfere with learning. Physical disabilities can be caused by many factors. Neurological impairments and diseases are the major causes described by the authors.   Other issues also addressed are the many technological advances that have facilitated these individuals' development and independence; realistic career choices; and socio-sexuality.

CHAPTER OBJECTIVES

On completion of this chapter, the student should be able to discuss the following topics:

1. The neurological and musculoskeletal conditions that lead to physical disabilities
2. The characteristics and categories of both neurological and musculoskeletal conditions
3. Other physical conditions, such as congenital malformations, accidents, diseases and abuse, that can result in a physical disability
4. A teacher's responsibility regarding child abuse and neglect
5. How the reactions to a disability can have a profound psychological influence on a disabled individual
6. The uses and limitations of prosthetics, orthotics, and adaptive devices for daily living

7. Educational placement options, educational goals, and curriculum for physically disabled students
8. The significance of the early intervention
9. The crucial and sensitive issues that will accompany the transition into adulthood
10. Some general strategies for the classroom teacher in order to facilitate effective instruction of physically disabled students

TERMINOLOGY

Terms To Note:

The following terms are important to note. These terms will be used in a Fill-In-The-Blank exercise at the conclusion of this chapter.

1. physical disabilities (p.344)
2. congenital anomalies (p.344)
3. cerebral palsy (p.347)
4. epilepsy (seizure disorder) (p.350)
5. spina bifida (p.353)
6. myelomeningocele (p.353)
7. myopathy (p.356)
8. atrophy (p.356)
9. muscular dystrophy (p.356)
10. rheumatoid arthritis (p.357)
11. osteoarthritis (p.358)
12. teratogens (p.359)
13. German measles (rubella) (p.359,360)
14. fetal alcohol syndrome (p.360)
15. AIDS (p.362)
16. battered child syndrome (p.366)
17. prosthetic (p.371)
18. orthotic (p.371)
19. adaptive devices (p.371,373)
20. hospital instruction (p.379)
21. homebound instruction (p.379)
22. positioning (p.381)
23. handling (p.381)

MULTIPLE CHOICE

Select the most appropriate response.

A. Remembering the Facts

1. The needs of many students with physical disabilities are not being met because: (p.345,346)

    a. the number of physically disabled individuals is increasing.
    b. there are very few qualified teachers for this population.
    c. health programs to assist the physically disabled are not growing at the same rate as the prevalence of this population.
    d. both a and b
    e. both a and c

2. Damage to the brain or spinal cord can cause: (p.346)

    a. mental retardation and learning problems.
    b. speech/language disorders and seizures.
    c. emotional disturbance, lack of coordination, and attentional difficulties.
    d. both a and b
    e. all of the above

3. When there is an indication that an individual's central nervous system has been damaged, one can almost always guarantee that: (p.346)

    a. muscular weakness and/or paralysis will be present.
    b. cognitive functioning will be delayed.
    c. he/she will have behavioral problems.
    d. speech and language development will be very delayed.
    e. he/she will be incapable of feeling or moving most parts of the body.

4. The average tested intelligence of individuals with cerebral palsy is: (p.350)

    a. in the lower than normal range.
    b. within the normal range.
    c. in the above normal range.
    d. in the severe range of retardation.

5. The most frequent age of onset of epilepsy is: (p.350)

    a. between birth and six years of age.
    b. before age 10 or after age 25.
    c. prior to adolescence.
    d. before six years of age or in old age.
    e. during adulthood.

6. Seizures do not present a major problem in a classroom because: (It is important, however, for a teacher to know how to respond should one occur.) (p.352)

    a. seizures are generally controlled either completely or partially by medication.
    b. students with a seizure disorder are not usually enrolled in most general classrooms.
    c. seizures most often occur during sleeping hours.
    d. students with seizure disorders usually wear protective helmets to help prevent injury.

7. Which of the following is NOT necessarily a characteristic of Spina Bifida? (p.353,354)

    a. a degree of paralysis
    b. loss of sensation and function below the site of defect
    c. nerve damage
    d. subnormal intellectual ability

8. Which of the following are musculoskeletal conditions? (p.356,357)

    a. muscular dystrophy and arthritis
    b. arthritis and epilepsy
    c. cerebral palsy and muscular dystrophy
    d. muscular dystrophy and spina bifida

9. Which of the following terms applies to a condition that is hereditary and progressive? (p.356)

    a. atrophy   c. palsy
    b. myopathy   d. dystrophy

10. For children with musculoskeletal conditions in which there are no additional exceptionalities, special provisions would only be necessary for the purpose of all of the following EXCEPT: (p.358)

    a. ensuring proper posture and positioning.
    b. providing mobility assistance.
    c. providing curriculum modification.
    d. providing homebound education if necessary.
    e. ensuring that the educational experience is as normal as possible.

11. Congenital defects occur in ___ of live births. (p.358,359)

   a. .5%   c. 5%
   b. 3%   d. 10%

12. The most frequently used teratogenic drug during pregnancy is ___. (p.359,360)

   a. alcohol   c. caffeine
   b. thalidomide   d. an antibiotic

13. The most frequent cause of infant mortality is ___. (p.361)

   a. congenital malformations
   b. fetal alcohol syndrome
   c. childhood diseases
   d. accidents

14. The authors report that approximately _____ of our population will be abused at one point during childhood. (p.367)

   a. 10%   d. 40%
   b. 20%   e. 50%
   c. 30%

15. Which of the following statements is TRUE regarding child abuse? (p.369)

   a. Nonhandicapped children are more at risk than
      handicapped children.
   b. Handicapped children are more at risk than
      nonhandicapped children.
   c. Both handicapped and nonhandicapped children are
      equally at risk for abuse.
   d. Handicapped children are rarely abused.

16. In considering the use of prosthetics, orthotics, and adaptive devices for daily living, which of the following is NOT a major consideration? (p.371-374)

   a. materials from which the device is constructed
   b. use of the individual's residual function
   c. simplicity
   d. reliability

17. According to the authors, one of the MOST important factors to be considered when a physically disabled individual chooses a career is ___. (p.385)

    a. intellectual level
    b. realistic expectations and aspirations
    c. high motivation
    d. availability of jobs
    e. emotional stability

18. Which of the following statements is FALSE concerning the sexuality of physically disabled individuals? (p.386)

    a. They have sexual needs which should be allowed to be gratified.
    b. Perhaps all that most physically disabled individuals can expect to experience is platonic relationships and sexual fantasies.
    c. Some physically disabled individuals can realistically expect marriage and children.
    d. It may be necessary to teach physically disabled individuals alternative methods of sexual expression and gratification.

B. Understanding the Facts

19. Jason sustained a spinal cord injury that resulted in paralysis of his legs and arms. Jason's condition would be referred to as: (p.348)

    a. hemiplegia   c. quadraplegia
    b. dyplegia   d. paraplegia

20. The difference between 'having a seizure' and 'having epilepsy' is one of ___. (p.350)

    a. intensity   c. duration
    b. frequency   d. age

21. An important procedure for a teacher to remember should a student have a seizure during class is: (p.352)

    a. Call a doctor.
    b. Do not attempt to stop the seizure. Let the seizure run its course.
    c. Never allow the student to sleep or rest after a seizure.
    d. Utilize mouth-to-mouth resuscitation if it appears that breathing has ceased.

22. A teacher's responsibility as it pertains to child abuse and neglect is: (p.366-368)

    a. to assist in detecting child abuse.
    b. to assist in reporting child abuse.
    c. to assist in preventing child abuse.
    d. all of the above
    e. a and b only

23. Jesse has spina bifida. He can walk independently with a very stiff gait. His spina bifida is accompanied by hydrocephalus. He has no cognitive deficit due to his condition. According to the authors, which of the following would assist Jesse the MOST in adapting and adjusting to his physical disability? (p.369-371)

    a. good medical attention
    b. appropriate school placement
    c. an effective affective education program throughout his academic career
    d. the reactions and acceptance of his family, his peers, and the public

24.   What is the reason for encouraging a physically disabled individual to utilize any residual function? (p.372,373)

    a. He/she will become more independent.
    b. He/she will become more efficient in movement and function.
    c. Through use, the affected limb(s) or body part(s) will be less susceptible to further deterioration and atrophy.
    d. a and b only
    e. all of the above

25. Which of the following factors is the LEAST significant when considering an educational placement for a physically disabled student? (p.374,379)

    a. mode of transportation to school
    b. type of disability
    c. severity of disability
    d. availability of community services
    e. medical prognosis for the condition

C. Applying the Facts

26. Carol has become temporarily disabled due to an accident. She will be spending several months in the hospital followed by additional recuperation at home. Which type of educational programming within the continuum of educational services would be least restrictive for Carol? (p.379)

    a. regular classroom with resource assistance
    b. self-contained classroom
    c. residential setting
    d. hospital/homebound instruction
    e. special day school

MATCHING

Match each of the following physical disabilities with the most accurate description.

a. hemiplegia (p.348)
b. diplegia (p.348)
c. quadriplegia (p.348)
d. paraplegia (p.348)
e. pyramidal (p.348)
f. seizures (p.350-352)
g. hydrocephalus (p.353)

h. scoliosis (p.358)
i. athetosis (p.381)
j. contractures (p.381)
k. asymmetrical tonic neck reflex (p.382)
l. hypotonia (p.382)

1. __E__ is a type of brain damage that can result in *spastic* movement.
2. __C__ is a type of CP resulting in legs and arms being either paralyzed or experiencing motor disability.
3. __H__ is identified by an abnormal curvature of the spine.
4. __L__ is identified by floppy and weak muscle tone.
5. __A__ is a type of CP resulting in one-half of the body being either paralyzed or experiencing motor disability.
6. __K__ is usually seen in normal babies between birth and four months and is considered abnormal after that developmental stage.
7. __J__ is a muscle tone problem that can result in permanent shortening of the muscles and connective tissue.
8. __D__ is a type of CP that results in paralysis or a disability in the legs only.
9. __F__ are a result of an abnormal discharge of electrical energy in certain brain cells and can influence level of consciousness and movement.

10. __B__ is a type of CP resulting in motor disability or paralysis in legs and arms, however, the legs are more extensively damaged than the arms.

11. __G__ can accompany spina bifida and is caused by excessive pressure of the cerebrospinal fluid.

12. __I__ is a muscle tone condition that results in almost constant uncontrolled movement.

TRUE AND FALSE

Indicate whether the following statements are True or False. In your notebook, rewrite the False statements so that they are accurate.

1. According to the textbook, children who are sensory impaired would not be considered to be physically disabled. (p.344)   T   (F)

2. Cerebral palsy is caused by a genetic disorder.   (p.278)
T   (F)

3. Individuals with cerebral palsy often have multiple handicaps.   (p.348,349)   (T)   F

4. Seizures usually follow a basic pattern with respect to frequency, duration, and type of movement.   (p.351)   (T)   F

5. In most cases, the causes of epilepsy are unknown. (p.351)   (T)   F

6. Spina Bifida can be surgically corrected.   (p. 353,354)
T   (F)

7. Arthritis can be found in individuals of all ages. (p.357)   (T)   F

8. AIDS presents problems for education, particularly for special education.   (p.362,365)   (T)   F

9. Every state has a law requiring a teacher to report cases of child abuse or neglect.   (p.366-368)   (T)   F

10. Research has suggested that there are personality 'types' associated with specific physical disabilities. (p.369)   T   (F)

11. For a student with a disability that is only physical, academic objectives should be the same as for a nondisabled student.   (p.369)   (T)   F

12. Because an individual is disabled, he or she has no need or ability for sexual expression. (p.386)   T   (F)

SHORT ANSWER QUESTIONS

Answer the following questions in your notebook.

A. Remembering the Facts

1. What are some of the reasons for the increase in the prevalence of physical disabilities within the past two decades? (p.345,346)

2. List four common causes of seizures. (p.351)

3. Discuss the various dimensions that differentiate among seizure disorders. (p.351)

4. What are some of the characteristics of muscular dystrophy? (p.356,357)

5. List five signs of child abuse that could be detected by a teacher. (p.366-368)

6. What are two reasons why many physically disabled students fall behind their peers in academic achievement? (p.369)

7. Review the five factors that are responsible for the increased public awareness and acceptance of physically disabled individuals. (p.369,370)

8. What are two major concerns of those who work with young physically disabled children?   Why are these concerns justified? (p.381)

9. What are seven factors that must be taken into consideration when a disabled individual investigates various career options? Which one of these factors do the authors suggest as the MOST important? (p.385,386)

B. Understanding the Facts

10. Provide two or three statements that would summarize what you now understand regarding the intellectual capacity of individuals with cerebral palsy. (p.349,350)

11. What is the significance of including a section on 'Adolescent Pregnancy' within a chapter on physical disabilities in a special education textbook? (p.365)

12. List six 'warning signs' that could indicate to a teacher that a potential physical problem exists? (p.381)

C. Applying the Facts

13. Ross, age 13, is classified as hemiplegic as the result of cerebral palsy. He also has a moderate hearing loss which has impacted on speech and language development. Provided with the information on cerebral palsy within this chapter, summarize four or five factors that should be considered significant for a teacher to address in implementing an educational program for Ross. (p.348-350)

14. Suggest ways in which a teacher can facilitate feelings of self-acceptance and adjustment in a physically disabled student. (p.369-371)

15. Suppose a child with a seizure disorder has been admitted to your classroom. Describe how you would prepare the other students for this new member. (p.350-353)

16. Prepare the arguments that would most likely be presented at a debate entitled: "Should students with AIDS be excluded from school?" Individuals to consider in such a debate would be the parents of the student with AIDS, other parents, other students, the teacher, and the student with AIDS. (p.362,365)

17. Why is abuse among handicapped children so prevalent? Can you suggest ways in which a parent could be assisted with this problem? How can the school assist abusive parents? (p.369)

18. This chapter has provided many practical suggestions for general classroom teachers. Construct five statements that would reflect some of the important considerations you have learned throughout this chapter. How will these five statements guide your planning should a physically disabled student be placed within your classroom?

FILL-IN-THE-BLANKS

Fill in the number of the most appropriate term listed under
'Terms to Note' for each of the following statements.

1. When the spinal column does not entirely fuse during
fetal development, _5_ is the resulting condition.

2. Jerry was seriously burned in a home accident. He will
be in the hospital for most of his fourth grade. As soon as
Jerry has recovered to a certain point, he should be
eligible for _20_ .

3. Susan wears a leg brace due to cerebral palsy. Marlene
was in an accident and now uses an artificial hand. Marlene
is utilizing a(n) _17_ , whereas Susan is utilizing a(n) _18_ .

4. Karen's mother contracted a serious infection during her
pregnancy. At birth, it was evident that Karen had suffered
moderate brain damage. She experiences upper body weakness
and uncoordination, as well as partial paralysis in her
lower body. Karen has _3_ .

5. Proper _22_ of a CP child in preparation for an activity
at home or at school would enable that child to function in
a more efficient manner.

6. _10_ is the most common form of arthritis among
handicapped children.

7. Rubella, or _13_ , is a very common teratogen.

8. Kevin, age six, has juvenile rheumatoid arthritis. At
times, his pain and swelling are so severe that he must stay
at home, sometimes for several weeks. Kevin would benefit
from _21_ in order to keep up with his school work.

9. The topic of _15_ would not have been addressed in an
introductory special education textbook a decade ago.
However, the authors cite a prediction that in the '90's, it
"will spare no school".

10. A baby with _14_ may experience growth retardation, brain
damage, heart failure, and/or hyperactivity. The mother's
behavior during pregnancy can completely prevent this
condition from developing.

11. _9_ is a hereditary disease that is characterized by a
progressive weakening and wasting of muscle fibers.

12. Children with __1__ are defined as those whose nonsensory physical limitations or health problems interfere with school attendance or learning to such an extent that special services and/or equipment are required.

13. Maureen's __4__ is manifested by momentary loss of consciousness and involuntary jerking of the limbs.

14. Rachel experiences extreme pain in her muscles. Her joints are often swollen and stiff. Rachel has __11__.

15. __8__ describes a condition in which neurological damage has caused a weakening of the muscles. __7__, alternatively, results in a weakening of muscles even when there is no evidence of neurological impairment.

16. Some children are born with a physical disability. A general heading for these disabilities is __2__.

17. Karen has osteogenesis imperfecta. Due to the fragility of her bones, a very important consideration in Karen's educational program would be one of __23__.

18. Betty's mother was exposed to German measles during the first trimester of pregnancy. As a result, Betty has several congenital malformations. The German measles virus is one of many __12__.

19. __6__ is a form of spina bifida.

20. Due to Donald's spastic movements and uncoordination, his parents have provided him with a 'spork' with a 'universal cuff', as well as a 'plate guard' to assist with mealtime independence. Donald is utilizing __19__ for daily living.

21. Sexual molestation, bruising, and neglect are all components of the __16__.

RETURN TO CHAPTER SUMMARY

Reread the chapter summary in the textbook (p.393-395) for a helpful review of all of the new information presented in Chapter Nine.

ENRICHMENT ACTIVITIES

For your interest and further study...

1. Visit with a family who has a physically disabled child. Take note of the special adaptations that have been made. Also, inquire concerning the family reactions, school adaptations, stress, and coping mechanisms that have accompanied this disability. From what you have learned from this experience, what words of advice could you provide parents who are just beginning to face the joys and difficulties of a newborn with physical disabilities?

2. View the 1970's movie, *Coming Home* with Jane Fonda and Jon Voight. Subsequent to watching this production, write some statements that would reflect your reactions and your learning regarding the sexuality of physically disabled individuals.

3. Consult with the administration of your local school system in order to determine child abuse reporting policies.

10

Giftedness

CHAPTER FOCUS

Even though giftedness does not *fit* the typical model of exceptionality (diagnose, prescribe, and remediate), it does *fit* with difficulties encountered with definition and identification. The authors address these concerns, in addition to an ongoing debate concerning appropriate programming for these students.

CHAPTER OBJECTIVES

On completion of this chapter, the student should be able to discuss the following topics:

1. The multiple-criterion definition of giftedness
2. The genetic and environmental origins of giftedness
3. Basic screening and identification procedures
4. The characteristics of gifted children
5. The characteristics and needs of neglected groups of gifted children
6. Educational approaches to gifted students
7. The attributes of an effective teacher of gifted students
8. General suggestions and strategies for teaching gifted children in a general education classroom and/or within a community school

TERMINOLOGY

Terms To Note:

The following terms are important to note. These terms will be used in a Fill-In-The-Blank exercise at the conclusion of this chapter.

1. precocious (p.400)
2. insight (p.400)
3. genius (p.400)
4. talent   (p.400)
5. creativity (p.400)
6. giftedness (p.400)
7. enrichment (p.426)
8. acceleration (p.426)

MULTIPLE CHOICE

Select the most appropriate response.

A. Remembering the Facts

1. Why are intelligence tests no longer the sole criterion for defining giftedness? (p.400,401)

   a. Above average intellectual functioning is not
      essential in order to be identified as gifted.
   b. IQ tests do not reliably or validly assess insight
      and creativity.
   c. IQ tests are not valid or reliable.
   d. IQ tests do not adequately assess deductive thinking.

2. The conceptual model of giftedness proposed by Horowitz and O'Brien suggests a dynamic relationship between ___.
(p.404)

   a. child and teacher
   b. IQ level and creativity
   c. environment and IQ level
   d. child and environment
   e. talent and motivation

3. Which of the following is NOT a significant factor within the definition of giftedness for the purpose of education? (p.406)

    a. high achievement   c. high task commitment
    b. high ability   d. high creativity

4. Gifted students were at one time identified solely on the basis of intelligence test scores. More recently, a(n) ___ approach is being utilized for identification. (p.411)

    a. achievement   d. case study
    b. I.E.P.   e. curriculum-based
    c. creativity

5. According to Renzulli and Delcourt, which of the following are essential criteria for identifying gifted students? (p.411)

    a. short term and long term creative productivity
    b. test scores
    c. academic mastery
    d. a and b only
    e. all of the above

6. Fostering growth in which type of program(s) does the American public appear to have the most support and interest? (p.422)

    a. music and art   d. drama
    b. athletics   e. science and math
    c. academics

7. Which of the following potential causes of underachievement in gifted students occurs MOST frequently? (p.423)

    a. social and cultural barriers
    b. lack of motivation
    c. assessment instrument inadequacies
    d. poor home environment
    e. inappropriate school programs

8. The authors report that many handicapped children and minority children are intellectually gifted. These students' cognitive abilities are often overlooked because of ___. (p.424)

    a. stereotypic expectations
    b. poor physical strength
    c. poor communication skills
    d. inadequate educational programming
    e. both a and b

9. Results from Stanley's SMPY study concluded that: (p.436)

   a. acceleration is beneficial for all gifted learners.
   b. acceleration is a better choice for learners who are precocious in areas of study requiring reasoning that is independent of social experiences.
   c. acceleration is a better choice for learners who are precocious in verbal and social areas.
   d. acceleration is not as beneficial as enrichment.
   e. enrichment is beneficial for all gifted learners.

10. Modification of the regular school curriculum for the purpose of making time for students to pursue alternative learning experiences is known as ___. (p.438)

   a. the case study approach
   b. the Revolving Door approach
   c. curriculum compacting
   d. Schoolwide Enrichment
   e. self-directed learning

B. Understanding the Facts

11. In which way is giftedness DIFFERENT from other exceptionalities? (p.398)

   a. Giftedness is something to be fostered.
   b. Giftedness has low prevalence estimates.
   c. It is easier to plan educational programs for gifted students.
   d. Giftedness does not produce social/emotional distress.

12. Which of the following would be an example of an enrichment program for gifted students? (p.430)

   a. The general classroom teacher employs a differentiated program of study without the assistance of a consultant.
   b. Gifted students are taught in a special school by specially trained teachers.
   c. Gifted students are grouped together for most of their school day and are taught by a special teacher.
   d. Gifted students leave the general classroom for short periods of time to receive additional instruction and challenges by a specially trained teacher.

13. Barry was given the opportunity to design and create his own concept of a community newspaper under the guidance of a local editor. This experience, according to the Schoolwide Enrichment Model, would be considered ___. (p.431)

    a. Type I   b. Type II   c. Type III

14. Mrs. Johnson's fourth grade class has spent every Thursday afternoon this year visiting or being visited by various professionals, business executives, and artists. According to the Schoolwide Enrichment Model, this experience would be referred to as ___. (p.431)

    a. Type I   b. Type II   c. Type III

C. Applying the Facts

15. Allen is an identified gifted student who resides in an isolated rural community. Twice each month, Allen's teacher receives state department assistance in designing an appropriate educational program for him. With which of the following educational plans is Allen's program consistent? (p.436)

    a. classroom enrichment
    b. independent study program
    c. consultant teacher program
    d. community mentor program
    e. resource room/pullout program

16. Sharon, age 16, is very interested in the fashion industry. She has already designed several formal dresses and is now entertaining some new ideas in designs for women's sportswear. A local sportswear fashion consultant has invited Sharon to work with her on the new summer line. This is an example of ___. (p.426)

    a. independent study program
    b. community mentor program
    c. classroom enrichment
    d. special school program
    e. consultant program

17. Carolyn is in second grade, She reads at an eighth grade level and can perform sixth grade mathematical operations. Biweekly, Carolyn leaves her class and joins other gifted students for accelerated study in selected curriculum areas. Carolyn is involved in a ___. (p. 426)

    a. resource room/pullout program
    b. special class
    c. community mentor program
    d. consultant teacher program
    e. enrichment in the classroom program

TRUE AND FALSE

Indicate whether the following statements are True or False. In your notebook, rewrite the False statements so that they are accurate.

1. The most accurate predictor of vocational and/or professional success is high intelligence. (p.401,403)
T   F

2. Renzulli's estimate of the prevalence of giftedness is the same as the federal prevalence estimate. (p.407)
T   F

3. Children who have been raised in a "better than average" environment by parents with "better than average" intelligence have a higher probability of being gifted than other children who have not had these advantages.
(p.408,409)   T   F

4. Genetics are more significant than environmental influences in the determination of giftedness. (p.408)
T   F

5. The fact that more males than females are designated as gifted is purely a biological factor. (p.408,410)   T   F

6. Giftedness is evident among children of all cultural and socioeconomic groups. (p.410)   T   F

7. Test scores are no longer used and are considered inappropriate in the identification of giftedness. (p.411)
T   F

8. As a group, gifted children appear to be similar, that is, they are superior in many ways. However, as individuals, gifted children show much variation. (p.414)
T   F

121

9. The terms *Underachievement* and *nonproductivity* can be used interchangeably. (p.423,424)   T   F

10. In order for a teacher to teach gifted students, his/her IQ must be in the gifted range. (p.432)   T   F

11. Independent study only involves a thorough exploration of a topic. (p.439)   T   F

SHORT ANSWER QUESTIONS

A. Remembering the Facts

1. Identify and discuss the three characteristics that define giftedness. Justify the inclusion of all three characteristics. (p.405,406)

2. Why do prevalence estimates vary so much? What may be some of the factors contributing to the lower prevalence estimate of gifted females? (p.407,408,410)

3. What do the authors cite as arguments against the statement: "...if gifted children are really so capable, they will find a way to help themselves"? (p.421)

4. According to Whitmore, what are three methods of increasing student motivation? How can a teacher use Whitmore's approach to assist with underachieving gifted students? (p.423)

5. What are the three characteristics of an effective educational program for gifted and talented students? (p.426)

6. What are the advantages and disadvantages of acceleration? For which students is acceleration more advantageous? (p.427,430,436)

7. Briefly outline the 'Revolving Door Model' of enrichment. (p.430,431)

8. What are the goals of self-directed learning? List and briefly describe the four components of self-directed learning. (p.438-440)

B. Understanding the Facts

9. How does giftedness relate to Darwin's theory of *survival of the fittest?* How can the concept of *fittest* be defined? Does it have similar meanings for everyone? (p.400)

10. Provide two or three statements that indicate what current research suggests as to the origins of giftedness. (p.407-411)

11. What are the advantages of a case study approach in identifying gifted students? How does this method assist with minority students? with underachieving students? with handicapped students? (p.400,401,411)

12. Explain the difference between a *gifted person* and *gifted behavior.* (p.403-406)

13. What reason would there be for such a large discrepancy between the federal estimate of prevalence of giftedness (3-5%) and Renzulli's estimate (15-25%)? (p.407)

14. Using "The Eight Great Gripes of Gifted Kids (p. 418) and "Being Gifted: Some Unhappy Feelings" (p.419), discuss the social and emotional problems that gifted children could experience. Compare and contrast these problems to those encountered by other exceptional children (learning disabled, mentally retarded, etc.).

C. Applying the Facts

15. Utilizing physical, educational, behavioral, social, emotional, and moral characteristics of gifted children, construct a profile on what a gifted child might 'look like'. (p.412-420,437)

16. What would be the value of a community mentor program at the secondary level? Suggest ways to establish this type of program in a school. (p.426,436)

17. What advice would you give to a parent of a gifted child? How could this parent maximize this child's potential? (p.433-435)

18. Based on the information provided within this chapter, what appear to be the most significant problems faced by educators responsible for gifted students?

19. This chapter has provided many practical suggestions for general classroom teachers. Write five statements that reflect what you have learned about gifted and talented individuals. How will this information guide your planning and teaching should a gifted student be placed within your classroom?

FILL-IN-THE-BLANKS

Fill in the number of the most appropriate term listed under <u>Terms To Note</u> for each of the following statements.

1. Steven, age four, cannot read the instructions or suggestions that have been enclosed within his construction toy sets. Steven's ___ allows him to look at several pictures of airplanes, helicopters, and cars in order to enable him to build a 'vehicle' that combines various features from each machine.

2. A combination of cognitive superiority, creativity, and 'stick-with-it' behavior that makes an individual distinctive is referred to as ___.

3. Placing gifted students ahead of their age-peers is known as ___, whereas providing supplementary materials, opportunities, and/or experiences for gifted students within the same environment as their age-peers is referred to as ___.

4. Melanie became an accomplished pianist by age four. By this time, she had also learned how to read and could spell words from her sister's fourth grade spelling text. Melanie could be referred to as ___.

5. Kevin has a 'flare for the dramatic'. He is a member of his secondary school drama club and has won awards for his outstanding portrayal of 'older gentlemen' in several school productions. Kevin has a dramatic ___.

6. A famous native artist was 'overtrained' in depicting native Americans in a western style. Recently, she has rebelled against her training and has demonstrated her ___ by combining geometric shapes represented in nature with spiritual images.

7. A rare talent in a particular aptitude is referred to as ___.

RETURN TO CHAPTER SUMMARY

Reread the chapter summary in the textbook (p.477) for an effective review of the information presented on the topic of Giftedness.

ENRICHMENT ACTIVITIES

For your interest and further study...

1. Read an autobiography or biography of an artist or writer who would be considered *gifted*. Focus on early childhood experiences that may have contributed to his/her accomplishments.

2. Interview some gifted students in order to determine the activities that are valued in the regular classroom and in the resource room.

11

Parents and Families

CHAPTER FOCUS

The concluding chapter of this text explores the significant and dynamic nature of the institution of *family*. A perceptive teacher understands the reciprocal impact that an exceptional child and his/her family have on each other. Due to the recent trend toward increased family involvement in the education of exceptional children, it is essential that teachers learn *how* to work with the family. Throughout this chapter, the authors stress the wealth of information and support that can be shared through an effective communication system between home and school.

CHAPTER OBJECTIVES

On completion of this chapter, the students should be able to discuss the following topics:

1. Earlier perspectives on parental roles and how these perspectives have changed
2. The various reactions of parents and siblings to the presence of exceptional children in the home
3. The family's critical role in the educational process
4. The difference between the Family Systems Approach and the Social Support Systems Approach to family involvement in treatment and education
5. Methods of effective communication between home and school

MULTIPLE CHOICE

Select the most appropriate response.

A. Remembering the Facts

1. In recent years, why have professionals become less likely to blame the parents for the problems encountered by their children? (p.447,448)

    a. Parents are not the cause of problems.
    b. Causes of problems are usually reciprocal in nature.
    c. Solutions for problems can often be found by enlisting the assistance of families.
    d. both b and c
    e. both a and b

2. Which of the following statements is TRUE concerning the Individualized Family Service Plan (IFSP)? (p.448)

    a. It is included in PL 99-457.
    b. It is included in Pl 94-142.
    c. It specifies services that need to be provided by the family in order to enhance the child's development.
    d. both a and b
    e. both a and c
    f. all of the above

3. Concerning parental reactions to learning that they have a disabled child, which of the following is a component of the *Stage Theory Approach*? (p.449)

    a. Parents go through a series of stages similar to the stages that accompany a reaction to a death of a loved one.
    b. All parts of the family are interrelated, therefore, events affecting any one member will also have an effect on others.
    c. Families should be perceived from a life-cycle perspective.
    d. Informal groups of people can be more helpful to parents than more formal or professional groups.

4. One of the most prevalent parental reactions to an exceptional child is ___. (p.449)

    a. guilt
    b. anger
    c. denial
    d. fear
    e. sadness

5. Which of the following is NOT a component of Turnbulls' Family Systems Approach?   (p.458-463)

    a. family interactions
    b. family support systems
    c. family life cycles
    d. family characteristics

6.   *Cohesiveness*   and   *adaptability*   are   important considerations in ___.   (p.458-463)

    a. family characteristics
    b. family interactions
    c. family functions
    d. family life cycles

B. Understanding the Facts

7.   Some   researchers   have   proposed   that   parents   of exceptional children go through similar stages and responses as someone who is bereaved.   However, one response in a death situation is NOT typical of a parental reaction to an exceptional child.   This response is ___.   (p.449)

    a. guilt   d. fear
    b. anger   e. sadness
    c. denial

8.   The   current   attitude   concerning   increased   family involvement in the education of exceptional children is very positive and effective because: (p.455,458)

    a. parents are the child's first *teachers*.
    b. parents and other family members often have relevant
       insights into the child's characteristics and needs.
    c. parents and other family members usually have an
       established rapport with the child.
    d. a and c only
    e. all of the above

9. "Jonathan is severely hearing impaired and developmentally delayed; is being raised by a single mother along with three siblings; lives in a small city in a midwest state." According to Turnbulls' Family Systems Approach, of which component is this statement reflective? (p.458)

   a. family characteristics
   b. family interactions
   c. family life cycles
   d. family functions

10. Ever since the family was young, Mom has always made breakfast and school lunches. Now the children are older and Mom has returned to her career on a part-time basis. The teenage son, who is refusing to arise a little earlier and make his own breakfast and lunch, is attempting to make Mom feel guilty for her new role. According to Turnbulls' family systems approach, the son is demonstrating a lack of ___. (p.458-463)

   a. rigidity   c. interaction
   b. cohesion   d. adaptability

11. Assisting families of exceptional children in becoming more independent and self-sufficient in providing physical and emotional needs will ultimately assist this family in all of the following areas EXCEPT: (p.456,457)

   a. gaining a sense of control.
   b. increasing self-esteem.
   c. developing a sense of competence.
   d. becoming more dependent upon more formal sources of support.

12. The most important component of an effective and productive parent-teacher partnership is ___. (p.469)

   a. communication   d. creative teaching
   b. trust   e. friendship
   c. honesty

TRUE AND FALSE

Indicate whether the following statements are True or False. In your notebook, rewrite the False statements so that they are accurate.

1. The family physician is usually the first individual to determine that a disability/exceptionality exists. (p.447,449)   T   F

2. Early in the 20th century there was a tendency to think of *parents* as the primary cause of a child's disability or problem(s). (p.446-448)   T   F

3. Families have a legal right to be involved in their child's education. (p.448)   T   F

4. Siblings of an exceptional individual often experience emotions that parallel those of their parents. (p.452)
T   F

5. Families who do not actively participate in their child's educational programming are demonstrating negligence. (p.460   T   F

6. According to the Life-Cycle perspective, the most stressful times for families of disabled children are transition points between stages. (p. 461,463)   T   F

7. A major premise of the Social Support Systems Approach is to assist families in helping themselves. (p.458-469)
T   F

SHORT ANSWER QUESTIONS

Answer the following questions in your notebook.

A. Remembering the Facts

1. In general terms, describe the *reciprocal* nature of parent-child relationships. How can this relationship be effectively used in implementing programs for exceptional children? (p.447,448)

2. Briefly describe the four components of Turnbulls' Family Systems Approach. (p.458-463)

3. Briefly compare the *emphasis* of the Family Systems Approach to that of the Social Support Systems Approach. How can both approaches benefit the family? (p.458-469)

4. What benefits are provided by parent support groups? (p.468)

5. Summarize the characteristics of the two methods of communication between home and school as described by the authors. What are the benefits of each? What are some of the problems that could be associated with each of these methods? (p.470)

B. Understanding the Facts

6. In the life cycle component of Turnbulls' Family Systems Approach, why is *transition* such a delicate and critical issue for families of exceptional children? (p.461-463)

7. List the *parental rights* as established by PL 94-142. (Chapter 1 - p. 23-25)

C. Applying the Facts

8. Mr. and Mrs. K are in their late 50's. They have three grown children. Their fourth child, aged 19, has cerebral palsy and is severely mentally retarded. He is also confined to a wheelchair, is incontinent, and needs assistance with feeding. List the concerns that this family would have at this stage of their life cycle. What are some of the options that this family could explore? (p.461-463)

9. What are some of the essential skills that a teacher of exceptional children should aim to develop in order to facilitate an effective parent-teacher partnership with the families of exceptional children? (p.469)

10. From a teacher's perspective, what are the advantages or benefits of attempting to develop a healthy parent-teacher partnership? What are the advantages or benefits from the child's perspective? (p.469-476)

RETURN TO CHAPTER SUMMARY

Reread the chapter summary in the textbook (p.477) for a helpful review of the information presented on the topic of parents and families.

ENRICHMENT ACTIVITIES

For your interest and further study...

1. Prepare a list of parent support groups that could be sent to a physician's office in order to assist him/her with interactions with parents of exceptional children.

2. Approach a family therapist and inquire as to helpful reading material for teachers that would facilitate an effective family-teacher relationship.

ANSWER KEY

CHAPTER 1   EXCEPTIONALITY AND SPECIAL EDUCATION

MULTIPLE CHOICE

1. c	7. e	13. a	19. d
2. d	8. b	14. b	20. a
3. b	9. b	15. d	21. e
4. a	10. c	16. b	22. b
5. e	11. d	17. c	23. b
6. a	12. a	18. c	24. a

MATCHING

1. d	4. a	6. e	8. h
2. b	5. c	7. f	9. g
3. i			

TRUE/FALSE

1. F	4. F	6. F	8. F
2. F	5. F	7. T	9. F
3. T			

FILL-IN-THE-BLANK

1. 6	5. 2	9. 7, 8	13. 18
2. 14	6. 5	10. 13	14. 3
3. 1	7. 16	11. 17	15. 15
4. 11	8. 4	12. 10, 9	16. 12

CHAPTER 2   ISSUES AND TRENDS

MULTIPLE CHOICE

1. b	5. c	9. d	13. c
2. d	6. d	10. d	14. b
3. c	7. a	11. e	15. c
4. e	8. b	12. b	16. c

TRUE/FALSE

1. F	4. T	7. T	10. T
2. F	5. T	8. T	11. F
3. T	6. F	9. F	

FILL-IN-THE-BLANKS

1. 8	5. 6	9. 3	13. 5
2. 13	6. 4	10. 9	14. 15
3. 2	7. 14	11. 1	15. 7
4. 12	8. 10	12. 11	

CHAPTER 3   MENTAL RETARDATION

MULTIPLE CHOICE

1. d	9. d	17. b	25. a
2. a	10. c	18. a	26. b
3. c	11. b	19. a	27. e
4. c	12. d	20. c	28. f
5. b	13. b	21. c	
6. b	14. a	22. c	
7. e	15. c	23. a	
8. d	16. b	24. b	

TRUE/FALSE

1. F	4. T	7. T	10. T
2. F	5. T	8. F	11. T
3. T	6. F	9. F	

MATCHING

I. Genetic Factors

1. d	2. a	3. c	4. f	5. b	6. e

II. Brain Damage

1. h	2. k	3. a	4. d	5. i	6. b
7. e	8. j	9. g	10. f		

FILL-IN-THE-BLANKS

1. 10	8. 30	15. 24	22. 31
2. 18	9. 2	16. 1	23. 3
3. 28	10. 29	17. 32,33	24. 13,14
4. 6,4	11. 25	18. 16,17	25. 19
5. 22	12. 8	19. 12	26. 5
6. 11	13. 9	20. 21	27. 15
7. 23	14. 20	21. 7,26	28. 27

CHAPTER 4   LEARNING DISABILITIES

MULTIPLE CHOICE

1. b	7. b	13. a	19. d
2. e	8. a	14. d	20. a
3. d	9. d	15. d	21. b
4. d	10. b	16. a	22. a
5. c	11. b	17. d	23. d
6. b	12. d	18. e	24. b

MATCHING

1. b   2. g   3. e   4. a   5. c   6. f   7. d

TRUE/FALSE

1. F	4. F	7. F	10. F
2. T	5. T	8. T	11. F
3. T	6. F	9. F	

FILL-IN-THE-BLANKS

1. 16	9. 31	17. 20	24. 26
2. 29	10. 18,17,19	18. 9	25. 11
3. 2	11. 1	19. 4	26. 27
4. 28	12. 5	20. 33	27. 14
5. 24	13. 8	21. 10	28. 21
6. 3	14. 6,7	22. 13	29. 15
7. 25	15. 23	23. 30	30. 12
8. 22	16. 32		

CHAPTER 5   EMOTIONAL/BEHAVIORAL DISORDERS

MULTIPLE CHOICE

1. b	6. d	11. b	16. f
2. e	7. f	12. d	17. e
3. a	8. d	13. a	18. f
4. a	9. b	14. c	19. b
5. a	10. c	15. e	

MATCHING

1. c   2. a   3. d   4. e   5. b

TRUE/FALSE

1. T	5. T	8. F
2. T	6. T	9. T
3. F	7. F	10. F
4. F		

FILL-IN-THE-BLANKS

1. 22	6. 3	11. 8,5	15. 6
2. 1,2	7. 23	12. 9	16. 16
3. 7	8. 13,14	13. 11,12	17. 20,21
4. 17	9. 24	14. 25	18. 10
5. 15	10. 19,18		

CHAPTER 6   COMMUNICATION DISORDERS

MULTIPLE CHOICE

1. a	9. d	17. d	25. d
2. b	10. e	18. d	26. e
3. a	11. a	19. a	27. a
4. d	12. c	20. e	28. c
5. c	13. a	21. d	29. e
6. c	14. c	22. b	30. d
7. d	15. a	23. a	
8. c	16. e	24. f	

TRUE/FALSE

1. F	4. T	7. F	10. F
2. F	5. F	8. T	11. F
3. T	6. T	9. T	12. T

FILL-IN-THE-BLANKS

1. 10	5. 13	9. 12	12. 14
2. 4	6. 6	10. 15,16	13. 9
3. 11	7. 17	11. 7,5	14. 2
4. 8	8. 1,3		

CHAPTER 7   HEARING IMPAIRMENT

MULTIPLE CHOICE

1. a	7. d	13. d	19. d
2. e	8. c	14. a	20. c
3. b	9. b	15. b	21. c
4. a	10. b	16. b	22. b
5. c	11. a	17. c	23. b
6. a	12. c	18. c	24. d

MATCHING

1. c	2. f	3. d	4. a	5. b	6. e

TRUE/FALSE

1. T	4. T	7. F	10. F
2. T	5. T	8. T	11. F
3. F	6. T	9. T	12. F

FILL-IN-THE-BLANKS

1. 24	9. 5,6	16. 15	23. 34
2. 10	10. 3	17. 38,39	24. 4
3. 31	11. 35	18. 16	25. 9
4. 40	12. 33	19. 32	26.20,21
5. 1,19,18	13. 22	20. 25,26,27	27. 11,12,13,14
6. 37	14. 2	21. 17	28. 29
7. 30	15. 28	22. 23	29. 36
8. 7,8			

CHAPTER 8   VISUAL IMPAIRMENT

MULTIPLE CHOICE

1. b	6. b	11. d	16. a
2. a	7. e	12. a	17. a
3. c	8. b	13. b	18. b
4. b	9. e	14. b	19. a
5. e	10. e	15. b	20. d

MATCHING

1. g	3. a	5. b	7. e
2. c	4. h	6. f	8. d

TRUE/FALSE

1. T	5. F	9. F	13. T
2. F	6. T	10. F	
3. T	7. F	11. F	
4. T	8. F	12. T	

FILL-IN-THE-BLANKS

1. 15	7. 17	13. 29	19. 6, 10
2. 13	8. 19, 18	14. 23	20. 20
3. 21	9. 8	15. 27,28	21. 7
4. 5	10. 24	16. 9	22. 25, 26
5. 2, 1	11. 16	17. 3	23. 22
6. 12	12. 11	18. 14	24. 4
			25. 30

CHAPTER 9   PHYSICAL DISABILITIES

MULTIPLE CHOICE

1. e	8. a	15. b	21. b
2. e	9. d	16. b	22. e
3. a	10. c	17. b	23. d
4. a	11. b	18. b	24. e
5. d	12. a	19. c	25. a
6. a	13. d	20. b	26. d
7. d	14. c		

MATCHING

1. e   2.c   3. h   4. l   5. a   6. k   7. j   8. d
9. f   10. b   11. g   12. i

TRUE/FALSE

1. T	4. F	7. T	10. F
2. F	5. T	8. T	11. T
3. T	6. F	9. T	12. F

FILL-IN-THE-BLANKS

1. 5	6. 11	11. 9	16. 2
2. 20	7. 13	12. 1	17. 23
3. 17,18	8. 21	13. 4	18. 12
4. 3	9. 15	14. 10	19. 6
5. 22	10. 14	15. 8,7	20. 19
			21. 16

CHAPTER 10   GIFTEDNESS

MULTIPLE CHOICE

1. b	6. b	10. c	14. a
2. d	7. e	11. a	15. c
3. a	8. a	12. d	16. b
4. d	9. b	13. c	17. a
5. e			

TRUE/FALSE

1. F	4. F	7. F	10. F
2. F	5. F	8. T	11. F
3. T	6. T	9. F	

FILL-IN-THE BLANKS

1. 2	3. 8,7	5. 4	7.3
2. 6	4. 1	6. 5	

CHAPTER 11   PARENTS AND FAMILIES

MULTIPLE CHOICE

1. d	4. a	7. c	10. d
2. f	5. b	8. e	11. d
3. a	6. b	9. a	12. a

TRUE/FALSE

1. F	3. T	5. F	7. T
2. T	4. T	6. T	